STANDARDS
FOR
SUICIDE PREVENTION AND
CRISIS CENTERS

Official Publication of the American
Association of Suicidology

STANDARDS
FOR
SUICIDE PREVENTION AND
CRISIS CENTERS

Jerome A. Motto, M.D.
Richard M. Brooks, Ph.D.
Charlotte P. Ross
Nancy H. Allen, M.P.H.

Behavioral Publications
New York

Library of Congress Catalog Number 73-17029
ISBN: 0-87705-105-4
Copyright © 1974 by Behavioral Publications

BEHAVIORAL PUBLICATIONS
72 Fifth Avenue
New York, New York 10011

Printed in the United States of America
456789   987654321

Library of Congress Cataloging
in Publication Data

Main entry under title:
Standards for suicide prevention and crisis
centers.

1.Suicide--Prevention. I. Motto, Jerome A.
(DNLM: 1. Community mental health services--
Standards. 2. Crisis intervention.
3. Suicide--Prevention and control. HV6545
S785 1974)

HV6545.S75   364.1'522   73-17029

CONTENTS

FOREWORD

Criteria are everything. Without guidelines,
standards, touchstones, verities, measures of success, evaluations of performance -- then all of
man's activities wax and wane and truth becomes,
if not inverted, then illusory and unobtainable.
The concern with standards is a measure of responsibility. There can be no excellence without criteria
for attainment. That is why this book on standards
marks a coming of age -- a measuring up to responsibility -- of suicide prevention efforts in this
country.

It is not accidental that the authors of this
book are all successful suicidologists, each in his
or her own way. Especially interesting to me is
that this interest grew out of a consortium of half-
dozen suicide prevention agencies within a limited
geographic area (specifically the Bay Area of California) and that these efforts resulted from liter-
ally hours of discussion, with both give-and-take
evolving practical standards for actual practice
without the diminution of higher ethical and professional principles, which are of course also
standards.

What is proposed in this book are not only
standards of acceptable conduct but criteria for
both the _effectiveness_ of suicide prevention efforts
and the _effects_ of such efforts within the total
community. When one thinks of the criterion that

is most relevant to suicide prevention activities,
the one that immediately comes to mind is the un-
equivocal reduction of suicide rate within the community where the center is operating. The work of
Bagley and his associates in England demonstrates
that the introduction of a suicide prevention unit
within a community can have a positive effect in
reducing the suicide rate of that limited community.
Unfortunately, in this country the suicide prevention efforts are not as homogeneous as they are
in England (where the activities studied were the
nationwide efforts of the Samaritan group), so that
this kind of current sociological experiment is
not possible in the United States. Further, because
we know that the suicide rate depends on many kinds
of factors including socio-cultural, economic,
political, military -- as well as dyadic and intra-
psychic -- it is probably not possible to demonstrate
the effectiveness of suicide prevention activities
in such a heterogeneous country as our own. (What
is painfully clear in suicide work is that successes
can never be pointed out without sounding self-
serving, but that failures are evident for all to
see).

For these reasons and others I am especially
interested that what might be called "second order"
criteria for effectiveness of suicide prevention
activities have been included in this volume. These
include greater liaison with other mental health
agencies (such as hot lines and drug treatment
clinics), focusing on related community problems,
an increased interest in the mental health and
well-being of citizens, and even an increased ap-
preciation of the value and worth of each human
life.

The authors, Dr. Motto, Ms. Allen, Dr. Brooks
and Ms. Ross should be commended. They have worked
against great odds in a field which is admittedly,
on occasion, colored more by opinion than by fact.

But they have worked together to produce a book which, while not the last word, is by far the best word to date that we have on what standards for suicide prevention should be.

When I was Chief of the NIMH Center for Studies of Suicide Prevention I was concerned about the suicide prevention centers and the community mental health centers springing up throughout the country, many without adequate supervision and some without adequate thought and planning. During that period I received a number of audio tapes of actual suicide calls, sent to me, I assume, with pride of craftsmanship. But I was deeply dismayed, on occasion, to hear that some of them were in fact clear examples of rather poor practice. I could do little more than to write, telephone, visit, encourage, promote better selection, more rigorous training and constant supervision -- and worry.

It is for that reason among others that I am especially pleased that these standards are now available, and that they come not from government but from four members in good standing in the American Association of Suicidology. I am also pleased that these standards speak, not officially, but for the authors and for many in the field who are concerned with the quality of citizen care. Not least of all these authors have set for all of us a standard on how standards ought to be promulgated. I welcome this effort and commend it to each person who is presently functioning within a suicide prevention center and to each unit that is being contemplated.

Edwin S. Shneidman, Ph.D.

University of California at Los Angeles
August, 1973

PREFACE

The vigorous application and continued development of formal standards should strengthen the
role of suicide prevention and crisis services in
the overall system of resources available to the
public. This is an important role in that these
services represent the only large scale utilization
of trained citizen volunteers for the provision of
clinical services which traditionally have been
relegated to professionals. In this instance the
uniqueness is enhanced by the distinct likelihood
that the quality of service is higher by virtue of
its volunteer nature. In no other setting can one
find twenty-four-hour-a-day responsiveness to emotional distress by a person whose interest and
training are geared to precisely that response situation. Haughton has pointed out that by the volunteers' "refreshing willingness to assume at least
limited responsibility for obtaining proper and
appropriate assistance for a person in crisis," and
by their follow-up programs, they "recognize and
correct a gross deficiency in the health and welfare
structure of many communities," and further observes
that, "It is in the unrestricted nature of their
availability that one finds the unique, innovative,
and truely exciting dimension of these services."
(American Journal of Psychiatry 124:1692-1696, 1968).

Standards for suicide prevention and crisis
centers are yet to reach the definitive stage of
development enjoyed by traditional health-related

facilities. During this formative period our efforts have been directed toward providing guidelines for identifying issues that are most relevant
to standards, and specifying criteria that can be
used to evaluate those issues. The goals are to
foster and to recognize quality programs and services, in the belief that only by diligent implementation of standards can this be accomplished in
a systematic way. We look forward to the time when
a voluntary program of accreditation, based on these
guidelines, is established to further these goals
on a nationwide basis.

The preparation of this material has been a
stimulating experience on several counts, not the
least of which has been the virtual absence of pre-
existing guidelines that we could build upon, bor-
row from or take issue with. This is reflected in
the rather sparse bibliography provided at the end
of each chapter, since little has been published
about standards as such. We have restricted these
references primarily to reports which go beyond
the "how to do it" manual and the "how it is being
done" survey, in order to focus on how to evaluate
whether the quality of what is being done meets an
acceptable level of excellence.

The initial development of explicit standards
led us to the practical question of how to go about
gathering information with which to determine the
degree of compliance with those standards. We
found four readily available means:

1. Written material from the agency with
   which to document specific areas of
   compliance, for example the detailed
   composition of the agency's governing
   body, paid staff and volunteers.

2. Written and verbal statements of a
   responsible board member, executive

director or staff member.

3. Answers to specific, detailed, sequential questions calculated to permit a judgment regarding degree of compliance.

4. First hand observation and discussion of pertinent aspects of an agency program, carried out by an on-site evaluation team.

Once over the initial hurdles of getting the evaluation mechanism into motion and accepting the inevitable arbitrariness involved in determining some of the ratings, we found the actual process of assessing compliance with published standards an exciting interchange in which all participants benefit. In an atmosphere of mutual respect and trust the evaluation procedure is generally experienced as an intensive consultation session, without need for defensiveness or undue anxiety. The common goal of maximizing program effectiveness seems to serve as a unifying influence that enhances the experience for all participants. Details of our procedures in developing and implementing standards are reported in the Bulletin of Suicidology, NIMH, March, 1969 and Fall, 1971.

The preparation of this manual was aided immeasurably by the patient and skillful assistance of Jane Steinberg, who prepared the typescript in photocopy-ready form. We are also indebted to the sources of our appendices: The United Bay Area Crusade for the "Checklist of Management Practices and Program," Gwyndolyn Harvey for the "Characteristics of Volunteers," and Al Loeb for his outline of "Program Evaluation -- From Concept to Action." The editorial staff of Behavioral Publications has

been generous with expert advice and suggestions,
which we also gratefully acknowledge.

Jerome A. Motto
Richard M. Brooks
Charlotte P. Ross
Nancy H. Allen

CHAPTER ONE

INTRODUCTION

Emphasis on standards for Suicide Prevention and Crisis Centers signals a new era in suicide prevention work. Though the establishment of new centers deservedly continues to receive much attention, the primary effort of the 1960's toward "getting started" has now given way to more advanced goals.

Established centers, past the initial struggle for viability, find themselves focusing largely on the twofold need to upgrade their programs and to stabilize their role in the community. Still a third need, engendered simply by reaching maturity, is to fulfill the expectation that advanced centers will provide guidelines for the development of newer organizations.

The shift of emphasis from the mechanics of generating a service to evaluating the quality of an ongoing operation introduces the formidable element of value judgements, which suggests an impressive increase in self-confidence on the part of those Centers which are participating in this development. It also implies a laudable insistence by these Centers on continued scrutiny geared toward constant improvement of services.

In a number of instances, however, concern for standards has been intensified primarily by

the urgency of the need to stabilize the Center's
role in the community health care system. Some
suicide prevention services, originally established on a trial basis or in an era of relative economic prosperity, are finding themselves subjected
to intense critical scrutiny prompted by constric-
tion of sources of support. In the absence of hard
data to demonstrate degree of effectiveness, even
the mature centers are vulnerable. The issue of
standards emerges as one clearly demonstrable criterion for a healthy, hence desireable, facility.

The rationale for using established standards
as such a criterion might be stated in the following way: If a widely held view maintains that a
given procedure will produce a given end, then con-
sistently carrying out that procedure with a high
level of excellence will ultimately bring about
that end, _even if the means of measuring the outcome are unsatisfactory_. Applied to suicide prevention, we may be able to survive the harsh challenge of deceptive suicide rates, but we cannot af-
ford a questionable level of efficiency in carrying
out the procedures calculated to reduce those rates.

The Bay Area Association for Suicide Prevention first developed a statement of standards in
1969, in order to facilitate integrating the activities of six suicide prevention and crisis centers in the San Francisco Bay Area. Subsequent application of those standards demonstrated their potential value for upgrading even well-established
programs, and for satisfying community demands for
assurance of the soundness of the organizations involved. Some of the material in this book stems
from this experience in the practical application
of standards to operating Centers, as well as the
authors' experience in providing suicide prevention
services and carrying out research in the field.

Though unique differences in local situations obviously deserve consideration in tailoring a suicide prevention and crisis service to a given community or geographic area, experience has taught that a number of overall principles are conducive to effective work in this field. Consideration of standards means nothing more than attempting to put these principles into practical and operational form.

At the same time there is much room for disagreement as to the generalizability of specific issues. For example, how crucial is it to provide face-to-face counselling, or to include follow-up services, or to include program evaluation as an integral part of a center's operation? Similarly, the division of standards into "Administration", "Staffing", "Training", "Service" and "Ethics" could be regarded as an arbitrary and restrictive categorization which overlooks more imaginative and effective approaches.

At the present stage of development there are four basic questions that must be answered in order to establish standards that are valid and have wide applicability as well:

Firstly, what are the broad categories of activity that we wish to evaluate? The efforts of the Bay Area Association for Suicide Prevention, mentioned above, provided some concrete suggestions which have been tested.

Secondly, what components within these broad categories lend themselves to quantifiable assessment? Again, the work already done provides a beginning which is elaborated in this book. Yet there are obvious gaps, such as rating the quality of performance of individual suicide prevention workers, which must be filled in as experience and validation of testing methods permit.

Thirdly, what criteria or instruments will serve as measuring devices for overall quality that are reliable, valid and feasible for general use? That is, what combinations of ratings add up to a level of excellence that permits a total center to be regarded as meeting a desired standard? This is a most troublesome task and doubtless the most controversial, especially insofar as judgements are introduced that are necessarily both subjective and arbitrary.

Fourthly, what are "minimal" as contrasted with "optimal" standards? All centers will have certain strengths and weaknesses. No limit is needed on strengths, but shortcomings require a definable point at which a "minimal" level can be identified. Where this point lies is understandably a sensitive issue, but one which cannot be avoided.

In spite of the complexities involved, the implementation of explicit standards has been demonstrated to be helpful both to the Center being assessed and to the evaluating agency. We hope that the discussions that follow will further the continued development of systematic procedures that will serve the need of all agencies engaged in suicide prevention and crisis-intervention efforts, not only to achieve and maintain the highest possible standards, but to demonstrate and measure them as well.

CHAPTER TWO

ADAPTATION TO THE SETTING

The establishment of an organization designed
to exert a preventive influence on suicide requires careful preliminary assessment of the elements in the local setting which are related to
this task. Such issues as community attitudes,
cultural patterns, available facilities and severi-
ty of the problem must be considered. Subsequently,
these elements must be carefully monitored to ascertain whether changes are required in the organization's procedures in order to pursue its goal
most efficiently. Means of doing this should be
built into the planning and ongoing stages of operation, including recording pertinent data and
documenting whenever possible.

Of course the nature of the specific characteristics involved varies with the geographical,
social, political and cultural setting of the area
to be served. Certain considerations can be generalized, however, and the application of standards
to this facet of a suicide prevention center's program refers to these broad areas of preliminary
evaluation and ongoing review.

There is a degree of overlap of this issue
with other considerations of standards, especially
"service standards," in that adaptation to the specific setting will be reflected in numerous aspects
of the center's organization and operations. Careful attention to this assessment of special charac-

5

teristics of the area to be served can thus serve
to alert one to other parts of the operation that
might otherwise be underemphasized. The following
specific questions are appropriate:

Has the extent of the problem in the area to
be served been carefully assessed? Evidence of
this assessment is found in data reflecting local
suicide incidence and rates (past and present) including long-term and short-term trends. Information about suicide attempts from police, hospitals,
physicians, emergency rooms and poison control centers can add to the picture in spite of the inevitable understatement of the total problem imposed
by unreported attempts. Indirect but related data
such as the prevalence of alcoholism, divorce, drug
addiction, requests for emergency psychiatric services and deaths from accidents are also pertinent.

Does the program allow for characteristics
inherent in a metropolitan, non-metropolitan urban
or rural area? For example, is there emergency
taxi service in the city and county or volunteer
transportation in the large rural areas? Are facilities geared to the college town, the one-industry
town or the community with a large proportion of
retired persons?

What are the attitudes of significant community
agencies? What are the attitudes as regards suicide
prevention services among the "professionals" in
the community, the police, fire department (rescue
services), local general emergency hospitals, community leaders, funding sources, political bodies,
city and county departments of health, medical and
psychiatric societies and private agencies? Some
evidence should be on hand reflecting awareness of
the importance of these attitudes, and efforts to
plan a program with them in mind.

What is the attitude of the coroner? To what
extent is the coroner interested in the problem
and willing to participate in special efforts to
supplement his certification procedure by such
measures as increasing post-mortems, routinizing
toxicology tests or cooperating in psychological
autopsies? Awareness of such possibilities and
steps to explore and implement them suggest a desired level of emphasis on this aspect of adaptation to the setting in which the center operates.
Of all the issues to be considered, the attitudes
and procedures of the coroner are most important
in clarifying the extent of the problem of suicide in a community.

What is the status of community relations?
Evidence of cooperation with police emergency units,
news media, telephone company, social welfare and
other pertinent agencies would suggest effective
integration of the community elements required for
efficient operation of the center.

What is the degree of integration with established mental health programs? This consideration
has been characterized by the Committee on Delivery
of Suicide and Crisis Intervention Services, of the
National Institute of Mental Health Task Force on
Suicide Prevention in the 70's, as "the greatest
weakness," "the first area to correct," "a major
reason for present inadequacies" and "the most
devastating criticism" of current programs. Such
strong language reflects, in part, the viewpoint
that crisis services are a health matter, and as
such must be integrated with -- eventually even
merged into -- the community's mental health system. This is not a universal view, however, and
local attitudes will determine the import of this
issue as a standard. Even the committee referred
to above grants the possibility that suicide and
crisis services are "neither health nor mental
health in nature," but that in any case they must

fit into "the community agency system" in a manner dictated by the unique circumstances and needs of the individual local community.

It seems clear that the identified functions of a center will largely determine its relationship to the health system. From the "suicide prevention center" model has of necessity evolved the "suicide prevention and crisis intervention" center, and the subsequent "crisis center." A parallel development, mostly outside the United States, has moved progressively further from the health related model with the "emergency telephone service," "distress center," "contact center" and finally the clearly non-medical "citizens advice bureau."

To the extent that integration with mental health agencies is needed in order to function effectively, this question will apply as a standard. Whether duplication of services exists or whether the service was developed primarily to serve the needs of the program organizers may be crucial considerations in priorities for funding, but the concern of standards is primarily quality of service, and this issue should be considered in that light.

BIBLIOGRAPHY

1. McGee, R., Berg, D., Brockopp, G., Harris, J., Haughton, A., Rachlis, D., Tomes, H., and Hoff, L.: The Delivery of Suicide and Crisis Intervention Services. In Resnik, H.L.P., and Hathorne, B., (Eds.): Suicide Prevention in the 70's. DHEW Publication No. (HSM) 72-9054, 1973, pp. 81-89.

2. Brockopp, G.: The Manpower Problem in Suicide
   Prevention Centers, or Programming the Sui-
   cide Prevention Center for Extinction. In
   Zusman, J., and Davidson, D., (Eds.): Organ-
   izing the Community To Prevent Suicide.
   Springfield, Ill.: C.C. Thomas, 1971.

3. Zusman, J.: Suicide Prevention, Crisis Inter-
   vention, and Community Mental Health Workers.
   In Zusman, J., and Davidson, D., (Eds.):
   Organizing the Community To Prevent Suicide.
   Springfield, Ill.: C.C. Thomas, 1971.

CHAPTER THREE

ORGANIZATIONAL STANDARDS

The ease with which the superficial aspects of a telephone crisis service can be offered to the public forces attention to the organizational makeup of such a service. Assurance of adequate controls and of ongoing scrutiny from a responsible administrative, professional, legal and fiscal standpoint are minimal requirements for organizational structure. This is usually achieved by assumption of sponsorship by an agency of unquestioned integrity backed by resources that assure availability of continuing supervision and guidance. Thus a church, health agency, university hospital or government facility is often involved. However, many telephone crisis services have set up their own organization from the outset, drawing on interested and qualified persons from many sources in the community.

As with other areas involving standards, precise means of accomplishing the purpose cannot be prescribed. Determining the best arrangement in a given community requires consideration of such matters as were discussed in Chapter One. The following questions can be considered further:

Is the local problem seen by the community as a public health issue? If so, affiliation with a public health agency would be appropriate. If not, a church or service organization may be more effective.

Are facilities readily available by virtue of
strong support from the established health care
system? For example, a community mental health
service, emergency service, medical emergency room
or ambulance service.

Will the attitudes of specific subgroups in
the community be crucial to the operation? Is
there a pre-existing, well established, interested
organization whose own ends will be served by sponsoring a crisis service, for example a religious,
educational, or labor institution?

Will any existing agency be unaccepting of a
crisis service by virtue of perceived overlap or
duplication of function? This may apply, for example, to a hospital emergency clinic, drug/hot-
line service or special problem agency whose clients may gravitate toward a 24-hour telephone service.

Whatever local circumstances and resources determine which organizational structure is most appropriate, it is important that ample allowance be
made for flexibility and innovation. Changing of
community attitudes, of key persons in the center
or in the community, or other changes can then be
adapted to with a minimum of disturbance to the service provided.

The following questions regarding organizational elements are pertinent to the implementation
of standards:

Nature of the Governing Board

Is there a Governing Board of some kind? A
Board of Directors is most common and in ordinary
circumstnaces is generally preferable. The govern-

ing board of the sponsoring organization, for example a church, mental health association, or hospital, can serve this purpose. However, whenever
possible it is most desirable to have an independent
board whose sole function is guidance and support
of the suicide prevention facility, in order to preclude diffusion of the suicide and crisis intervention issue.

What agency does the Board represent? Guidance by a responsible organization, of course, is
conducive to confidence in the stability and quality of the services provided. This cannot be taken
for granted, however, and possible conflict of interest with the sponsoring agency must be considered.
For example, does the parent organization sponsor
other projects that may compete for support? Does
it reflect some inflexible or doctrinaire values
that may handicap the facility in helping persons
with socially disapproved issues such as unwanted
pregnancy, drug abuse, or homosexuality?

Does the Board have written by-laws or other
prescribed procedures providing for such matters
as frequency of meetings, assignment of responsibilities, personnel policies and eligibility for
tax exempt status? A copy of the prescribed structure and procedures should be on hand for ready
reference and review. Each individual board member
should be aware of his specific responsibilities to
the Board and to the goals of the Center.

Does the Board provide a broad representation
of the community? Do minority groups, professions,
business, housewives and students have a voice?
Does the Board reflect awareness of the need for
involvement of important local interests for fund
raising, political strength and implementation of
program?

Evaluation of the Board's Function

How frequently does it meet? An active
"participating" Board in an innovative Suicide Prevention Center would probably have to meet at least
monthly, supplemented by interim committee work.
In such a Board, members may be expected to actively
participate in the ongoing programs of the Center.
If the Board sees its role as limited to supervision
and guidance, bimonthly meetings would probably suf-
fice.

What is the attendance at meetings? At least
a quorum should be present regularly. Attention
should be paid to habitual absentees, non-partici-
pating members or out-of-place members unable to
contribute to the task. Similarly the "workhorses"
deserve note, especially if one or two persons do
essentially all the work of the Board.

Are minutes kept? Evidence of a business-
like procedure is desirable, as well as a record
of pertinent considerations and a medium for com-
municating the Board's deliberations to other appropriate persons or agencies. Attendance and
participation of Board members are also reflected
here.

Is the Board kept informed of pertinent
matters? Letters, reports of activities and minutes of committees serve to channel necessary information to the Board and make it most responsive
to the needs of the Center.

Does the Board provide "directorship"? This
implies that substantive matters are presented for
guidance and development of policy. It is a crucial question that requires a subjective judgement,
which may be based on observation, discussion with
Center personnel and review of the Board's written
materials.

The question of standards, as applied to a
Board of Directors, clearly boils down to whether
a responsible ongoing review of a Suicide Prevention Center's activities is being carried out, and
whether effective participatory leadership and di-
rection is being provided. An excellent discussion
of this matter is given by J.W. Herring (1957),
which is directed to the general issue of board
leadership but is pertinent to the role of the governing board of a suicide prevention facility.

Professional Advisory Committee

Is authoritative professional advice readily
available to the governing body of the organization?
The constant need to consider technical and policy
matters involving such diverse areas as social agencies, religious issues and medical services necessitates organizational provision for guidance in these
matters. The membership of the Board of Directors
may itself satisfy this need. Ideally, however, a
Professional Advisory Committee would serve as a
consultative body to the Board on technical matters,
permitting the Board to focus on broader problems
of policy and services. In some instances this
might be in the form of an ad hoc subcommittee of
the Board, constituted when the need arises and
free to include resource persons who are not Board
members. A specific resource which should be established, and its availability assured prior to emer-
gence of a specific need, is the name of an attorney
who is available for an expert opinion on legal
questions.

Does the Professional Advisory mechanism fulfill its role? As in the preceding discussion of
the Board of Directors, the effectiveness of the
professional advisory mechanism is judged by docu-
mented evidence of its function. This implies records of committee membership, meetings, attendance,
matters discussed and recommendations made.

Executive Director

Is one person in direct charge of the operation of the facility? Unification of responsibility for a Center's day-to-day operations is conducive to efficiency and consistency, though of
course does not ensure it. Shared responsibility,
for example one person in charge of daytime coverage and another in charge at night, is certainly
possible, but such an arrangement can generate se-
vere problems of continuity and communication. If
more than one person is in an "executive director"
role, regardless of the specific job titles used,
special provisions should clearly define areas of
authority and assure clear communication.

Is the person in charge on a full-time basis?
This is highly desirable and in some instances
essential to achieve efficient operation. Of
course local conditions differ, and a full-time
person may seem extravagant early in a Center's
experience when relatively few calls are coming
in. It is the inability to predict when circumstances will require his presence that makes this
an important consideration. As in the preceding
question, if it is not possible to have a full-
time Director, special measures should be taken
to enhance communication and provide appropriate
support for the person on the telephone when the
Director is not present.

Is provision made for the Director to be informed and to play an appropriate role in all aspects of the Center's operation? Such provisions
might include, for example, having the Director
present at Board meetings, included in the distri-
bution of minutes (or participate as ex-officio
member) of committees, informed of developments
regarding such matters as program evaluation, staff
conflicts, research findings, unusually difficult
callers, etc. The personality of the Director and

other local circumstances will determine the arrangement in a given Center, but some organizational provision should be made to ensure that
the Director's function is facilitated. These
considerations involving the Director of the Center are an important aspect of the Center's organizational structure, and must be clearly differ-
entiated from the standards applied to the qualifications of the Director discussed in Chapter
Four.

Agency Records

An evaluating body may easily assume that the
quality of record keeping reflects the quality of
service provided by a Center. Though such an assumption may be fallacious, it is especially tempting because it is so much easier to assess records
than service. This pattern has a firm precedent
in the evaluation, for example, of hospital services.

Who keeps the financial records? This would
frequently be the Executive Director, though he
may delegate the actual bookkeeping task to another
staff member. The responsibility for the adequacy
of the records, however, would ordinarily remain
with the Director.

Where are the financial records kept? Both
availability and security are necessary, to facilitate prompt posting of entries and provision for a
business-like means of assuring accountability.

How systematically are the financial records
kept? The sensitivity of any community to financial matters necessitates readable, up-to-date
entries that observe recognized bookkeeping principles. This statement is too obvious to belabor,
yet it is far from universal in its application.

What operational records are maintained?
Minimal data on operations would include records
of calls to the Center with evaluation, followup
and disposition, personnel and shifts covering the
phones and other responsibilities, trainees and
training programs, public relations, educational
materials and monthly/yearly data pertinent to
program evaluation. It is desirable to also have
written statements of agency policies, procedures,
and job descriptions for agency personnel.

How available is the recorded information?
Ideally, of course, recorded material is up-to-
date, quickly retrievable and in understandable
form.

The specific forms required to record pertinent information vary according to the specific
services and goals of each Center. Examples of
forms utilized by a wide variety of suicide prevention and crisis intervention agencies are provided in the extensive appendices included in
Fisher's (1972) survey of these services in the
United States. Only one of these examples (Suicide Prevention Services, Indianapolis) illus-
trates a pre-coded form, which would seem to be
advantageous when analysis of the data is under-
taken.

A comprehensive set of statements which can
serve as a guide for the organizational aspects
of a center's program is provided in Appendix A,
"Check List of Management Practices and Program."
This set of "yes-no" items has been used by a
large funding agency with extensive experience in
evaluating soundness of organizational structure.
Though it may go beyond the needs of many suicide
and crisis intervention facilities, it can provide
a useful means of reviewing this issue from the
viewpoint of standards.

BIBLIOGRAPHY

1. Herring, J.W.: Creative Board Leadership.
   Adult Education Association of the U.S.A.
   Leadership Pamphlet No. 14, 1957, pp.15-18.

2. Fisher, S.A.: The Voice of Hope -- To People
   in Crisis. Canton, Ohio: Shiela A. Fisher,
   1972.

CHAPTER FOUR

STAFFING STANDARDS

The importance of having an effective, well-trained staff in suicide prevention and crisis centers is self-evident. Staffing, more than any other single factor, determines the level of excellence at which a service functions.

The staffing pattern of a suicide prevention center is usually determined by the types of services provided, for example, emergency telephone and referral service, drop-in facilities, or home visiting program. Ideally, the kind of service provided is determined by the needs of the community. Practically, the staffing pattern is largely determined by the resources available, that is, whether the staff is paid or volunteer, professional or non-professional. There is no single preferred pattern because the role of the Center necessarily varies in different communities. The standards suggested here are to assure a high level of service regardless of the staffing pattern used.

The non-professional volunteer has become recognized as the major source of manpower for the delivery of crisis services, especially for a 24-hour emergency telephone referral facility. Approximately 80% of suicide prevention centers utilize non-professional volunteers as the primary crisis worker. Using such volunteers in suicide prevention work is one method of mobilizing a community and extending suicide prevention into the community.

Both quality and quantity of staff members
are essential elements and are considered sepa-
rately in this discussion. The categories of
personnel to be considered are a) administrative
head of the service, b) teaching, training and
supervisory personnel, c) consultant staff and d)
volunteers or other persons who respond to crisis
telephone calls. Each person should have a clear
concept of his job, and should know specifically
what is expected of him as well as what he can
expect of others.

Some specific questions are as follows:

Administrative Head

What are the Director's academic qualifications? This implies formal teaching and training
in an academic course of study in a given discipline. It is preferable that this discipline be
related to mental health but is not essential.
Such areas as psychology, sociology, anthropology,
social work, health education, and medicine can
provide an appropriate academic background. Pre-
sumably the longer the duration of study the more
thorough the academic preparation will be, though
of course this cannot be taken for granted.

What are the Director's professional qualifications? This refers to his professional knowledge,
experience and demonstrated skills. These elements
focus more on practical than theoretical preparation, and generally deserve greater weight than
academic qualifications in determining the excellence of a staff. It is necessary to be very specific in assessing this qualification in order to
ascertain the relevance of his professional experience to responsibility for crisis services. That

is, how long has he performed what services in
what setting, at what level of excellence?

What are the Director's personal qualifications? This refers to such characteristics as attitudes, personality and motivation for crisis intervention work. It is without doubt the most important element to assess and deserves to carry
more weight than either academic or professional
background. At the same time, of course, a person
highly regarded for his personal qualities could
not function effectively as a Center Director on
these qualities alone.

What are the Director's administrative qualifications? This refers to training, experience
and demonstrated skills in organizational work, development and supervision of programs, administrative responsibilities, budgeting and public relations. Though difficult to assess, these aspects
of a Center Director's role are certainly important enough to warrant scrutiny. At the same time,
a lack of qualifications in this area may be made
up for by appropriate use of consultants, resources
from the Board of Directors or Professional Advisory
Committee, delegation of administrative matters to
a qualified assistant and the Director's own involvement with self-improvement and continuing education.

How knowledgeable is the Director about the
field of suicide prevention and crisis intervention
in general and the operation of his own Center in
particular? Such expertise is generated by the elements mentioned above to the extent that they are
directed toward work in the field of suicide prevention. While it is not essential that he have
facts and figures on the tip of his tongue, his
responsibility for seeing that appropriate records
are kept of the agency's operations should make it
possible for him to readily obtain pertinent data

about his own locality and agency activities. His
acquaintance with procedures and experience outside
of his own Center may be a reflection of his willingness to learn from others and to try out innovative approaches used elsewhere.

Has the Director demonstrated initiative and
resourcefulness in developing the Center's program?
The many obstacles that are usually encountered in
conducting a suicide prevention center often call
for creative thinking as well as dogged optimism.
Evidence of this capacity deserves consideration.

To what extent has the Director sought and
utilized community participation in the Center
program? No matter how talented a staff may be,
it requires community cooperation and collabora-
tion to operate effectively. Establishing such
working relationships with members of the ministry,
public health nurses, police, medical facilities,
telephone company, taxi companies and coroner repre-
sents clear evidence of effectiveness. The Director
has a responsibility to make the suicide prevention
service known to the community as well as to be
familiar with appropriate resources for referral.

The assessment of an Executive Director is
clearly a matter involving intuitive impressions of
leadership qualities, knowledge, personality, and
administrative ability, for which objective guidelines are difficult to establish. It tends to be
a very sensitive issue as well, especially if the
Director perceives the procedure as a personal assessment rather than a role evaluation.

Teaching, Training and Supervisory Personnel

What are the academic, professional, and personal qualifications of the teaching, training and
supervisory staff? It is perhaps too obvious to

state that these staff members should be qualified
for their role by reason of their own training or
appropriate experience. This may include knowledge
and experience in such areas as psychology, psychiatry, sociology, health education, pastoral
counselling, psychiatric nursing, psychiatric social
work and suicidology. It is most important that
their experience include the clinical application
of their training to the specific needs of a crisis
service. The most knowledgeable person, regardless
of his discipline, is severely handicapped as a
teacher or supervisor if he has not had experience
taking crisis calls himself. Generally, of course,
the longer and more extensive this experience the
better qualified he would be to appreciate the
training needs of new persons in the field. It is
essential that all teaching personnel be familiar
with the concepts and practice of suicide prevention,
including knowledge of community resources for referral purposes.

Personal qualities are difficult to assess but
are too important in the learning process to ignore.
Elements such as honesty, uncompromising integrity,
profound respect for fellow human beings, appreci-
ation of another's experience and empathic concern
for their discomfort lie at the very base of the
Center's work. Each trainee's potential for developing these qualities can be best realized by
the teaching and supervisory personnel exemplifying
them.

Consultant Staff

The consideration of consultation standards
assumes that every crisis worker, no matter how
well trained and experienced, is at times faced
with situations that would benefit from a consultant's view. This refers both to emergency situations that arise unpredictably, and to day-to-day
operations. In emergencies there is general agree-

ment about the consultant's role. In more routine
operations, however, we are concerned with the
tendency to settle into a pattern that is considered
satisfactory, and then to continue it, even though
circumstances may require change. The observation
that "some people keep repeating the same mistakes
over and over and call it experience" is the basis
for setting up safeguards in the form of a "scheduled"
as well as "back-up" consultation program.

Our assumption regarding need for consultation
applies to all persons directly engaged in crisis
work, regardless of their status as "paid staff,"
"volunteer staff" or "professional." Available resources may limit the implementation of this, but
its desirability should be recognized. Staff members should likewise be encouraged to use consultation -- whether to better deal with their own
feelings regarding their handling of crisis situations or regarding their specific services to
callers.

The crucial role of physical injury in self-
destructive behavior suggests the need for inclu-
sion of a medical consultant in an agency program.
The nature and degree of risk produced by the ingestion of various drugs, or the withholding of
needed medication such as insulin or digitalis,
typify the kinds of information that a crisis worker may need to obtain in order to adequately assess the suicidal risk of a caller or to formulate an
appropriate action plan. Some centers deal with
this by routinely referring the caller to a medical
setting regardless of the degree of risk, on the
premise that a crisis worker cannot and should not
attempt to evaluate it. Such an approach is sound
in some instances -- in others it can lead to los-
ing the caller. Some room for judgement permits
a modicum of flexibility, though in case of doubt
the "safe" procedure is certainly called for.

A physician who can provide immediate consultation about specific medical problems is thus desirable, though he would rarely be available around the clock. Therefore, a formal agreement with the staff of a 24-hour emergency medical facility should also be arranged, to assure availability of adequate medical consultation at all times.

Of course the qualifications of consultants must be considered as well as their existence and availability. Though this is obviously difficult to assess from a distance, criteria such as professional certification, opinions of Professional Advisory Committee members (especially from the same discipline), publications or experience in crisis work, and subjective impressions of the crisis workers can be utilized.

Some specific questions would be:

What are the academic, professional and personal qualifications of the consultant staff? Since consultants can be utilized for a variety of purposes, one should ask what specific expertise a given consultant offers to the Center. Many technical questions, for example the lethality of a given sleeping medication, can be erroneously answered by persons with little experience in suicide prevention work. Those consultants who provide "back-up" services would be expected to have had personal experience in the activity that they are consulting for. Thus it is necessary to clearly define the consultant's role in order to determine the qualities which must be assessed to carry out that role. A toxicologist, for example, would ordinarily be the most valuable resource for problems involving ingestion of drugs or other toxic substances.

How readily available is the consultant staff?
It is possible to present documentary evidence of
consultant resources that in fact are not readily
available to the person on the phone. Assessing
this issue could include a test call, or at least
asking telephone personnel what their experience
has been with given consultants rather than depend-
ing entirely on written assurance of availability.

How carefully are community resources screened
in the process of selecting consultants? It is not
unknown for a suicide prevention center to accept
the services of a consultant on the basis of the
consultant's interest in suicide prevention alone,
without careful assessment of his qualifications.
Thus in applying standards to a consultant staff
it is necessary to include in one's judgement the
care with which the consultant was selected. Is
he a member of the local professional group in his
discipline? Is he "certified" by his professional
organization? Have opinions been solicited from
his professional colleagues as to the appropriateness of his functioning as a consultant? Has he
manifested special interest in an instructional
role by serving as consultant to other local agencies or as a teacher in local professional schools?

Are emergency consultations available to the
telephone crisis worker at all times? Who serves
in this role? How are they reached? Is provision
made for further back-up if the consultant cannot
be located?

How frequently are consultants utilized?

Are consultant's suggestions recorded as such
for later reference?

How does the worker know whom to call (on a
schedule?, always the same person?, informed ver-
bally when coming on duty?)?

<u>What is the subjective view of individual
crisis workers as to the usefulness of their con-
sultations</u>?

<u>Are regular supervisory consultations sched-
uled for the crisis worker in addition to emergency
consultations? With whom? How often? How long
(duration)? Is it optional or mandatory? Is it
on a one-to-one basis? Are the objectives of the
consultation sessions clearly defined</u>?

Volunteers

<u>How are the volunteers selected</u>? The entire
issue of effective identification of appropriate
volunteers is still unsettled. At present it is
necessary to assess primarily the care with which
volunteers are recruited, screened, trained and
evaluated, granting that human error will enter
into the process no matter how carefully it is
done. Specific information would involve how initial contact is generated, how volunteers apply,
who interviews them, how many different interviewers are involved, the number and length of interviews, the qualifications of the interviewers, and
what other screening devices are utilized at what
stages in the selection program.

At least two qualified interviewers (prefera-
bly three) are desirable in the initial screening
process. Data regarding past and present life
patterns should reflect evidence of emotional stability, integrity, receptivity to learning, per-
ceptiveness and responsiveness to human needs.
Psychological testing, multiple interviews, role
playing and peer judgements of active volunteers
have all been used to advantage.

Among the personal experiences relevant to
screening a potential worker is the history of a

prior suicide attempt. Some centers consider this
ample reason for denying them direct involvement
in crisis calls, but find other kinds of tasks for
them to do within the Suicide Prevention Service.
It is highly advisable to give such individuals
serious consideration, as personal experience of
a suicidal nature can operate beneficially, lead-
ing to a greater depth of understanding. On the
other hand such experience may increase vulnera-
bility to the suicidal act. This is something the
interviewer must assess during the screening process, in the light of an explicit policy established
by the agency.

   Does the selection procedure involve a check
list of desirable qualities? Is there an indication
of how applicants are rated, for example, are ratings based more on specific information or on intu-
ition? A useful, down-to-earth list of both desirable and undesirable traits in volunteers, developed at the St. Louis Suicide Prevention Center,
is included in Appendix B.

   The use of such lists or other methods to improve selection procedures suggests a progressive
upgrading of efficiency and excellence of the volunteer staff.

   What is the rate of turnover of volunteers?
The range and mean duration of volunteer service
provides one measure of stability and of the likelihood that a volunteer staff is progressively achieve-
ing a higher level of effectiveness. Exceptions to
this certainly occur, but if other factors are
equal, a more experienced volunteer staff will certainly be more effective than a less experienced
one. Providing a continuing challenge and sense
of growth to experienced volunteers is one of the
tasks of the Executive Director that requires
creativity and innovation.

<u>What reasons are given by volunteers for leav-</u>
<u>ing the program?</u> Expressions of dissatisfaction
may offer clues to shortcomings in the Center's
program, weakness in the selection procedure, or
growth of the volunteers into new levels of functioning. Staff morale is enhanced by formal recognition or by support of attendance at suicidology
meetings and workshops. In order to maintain the
volunteer's job satisfaction he needs both involvement and recognition.

The assessment of staffing standards discussed
above reads in part like a recitation of the obvious.
Yet to overcome the ever-present manpower shortage
in crisis services the obvious is known to have
been overlooked. Below a certain level, staff inadequacies do the cause of suicide prevention more
harm than good. Our concern has been to assure adequate effectiveness of those persons who do carry on
the vital work of suicide prevention and to minimize
errors in the process of screening out those who are,
as Chad Varah has put it, "excellent citizens with
the wrong virtues." We have also tried to give adequate recognition to the value of prior living experience, professional training and experience, intuitive skills and common sense in the selection of
persons who will be trained to answer that special
telephone. They form the backbone of the suicide
prevention effort, and their selection deserves
maximum emphasis in assessing the staffing standards
of a crisis center.

BIBLIOGRAPHY

1. Heilig, S.: Manpower: Utilization of Nonprofes-
     sional Crisis Workers. In McGee, R. (Ed.):
     Planning Emergency Services for Comprehensive
     Mental Health Centers. Gainesville, Fla.:
     University of Florida, 1967, pp.46-53, 127-129.

2. Heilig, S., Farberow, N., Litman, R., and Shneidman, E.: Nonprofessional Volunteers in a Suicide Prevention Center. Community Mental Health Journal, 4:287-295, 1968.

3. McGee, Richard K., Staffing of Suicide Prevention Centers: Alternatives and Implications. In: Suicide Prevention Advanced Workshop-Procedings of a Conference, University of California (S.F.) and Suicide Prevention Center of San Mateo County, March 20-21, 1970, pp. 2-8.

4. Pretzel, P.: The Volunteer Clinical Worker at the Suicide Prevention Center. NIMH Bulletin of Suicidology, No. 6, Spring, 1970, pp. 29-34.

5. Randell, J.: A Nightwatch Program in a Suicide Prevention Center. NIMH Bulletin of Suicidology, No. 6, Spring, 1970, pp.50-55.

6. Varah, C.: The Use of Lay Volunteers in Suicide Prevention. In: Farberow, N. (Ed.): Proceedings, Fourth International Conference for Suicide Prevention. International Association for Suicide Prevention, 1968, pp. 90-96.

7. Brockopp, G.: Selecting the Crisis Intervener. Crisis Intervention 4(2):33-39, 1972.

CHAPTER FIVE

TRAINING STANDARDS

The training of suicide prevention and crisis
workers has developed largely as a reflection of
the needs of individual center programs and of the
training resources available to them. These programs range from simple telephone services using
volunteers working out of homes and/or an office,
to comprehensive programs offering 24-hour emergency telephone services, clinical services, community
outreach programs, and special problem services.
The staffs range from lay volunteers to paid professionals and include all combinations in between.
Thus a wide variety of training programs has necessarily evolved. Varied as these programs and
these staffing patterns are, some general guidelines have been recognized as conducive to effective training for this work, and essential for
those who engage in it.

It is important that _all_ suicide prevention
workers be included in the service's training program, regardless of their academic or professional
backgrounds. Some services which utilize psychia-
trists, psychologists, nurses, ministers or counse-
lors have felt that such professionals were already
sufficiently trained in dealing with troubled people. Additional training, in their opinion, was
unnecessary and perhaps even demeaning. Experience
has repeatedly indicated, however, that because the
task of the staff of a suicide prevention and crisis
intervention center is unique and specialized, spe-

31

cific training in this work should be required of
all who participate in it.

It is necessary to specify goals in order to
consider evaluating the effectiveness of a training program. In this instance <u>a body of factual
knowledge, specific defined skills, and a realistic set of attitudes as regards suicidal behavior</u>
are suggested as the general goals of a training
program in suicide prevention work.

The factual content of a training program
should cover at least the following topics:

Basic suicidology

The nature and extent (epidemiology) of the
problem of suicide and suicidal behavior -- in
general and as it relates to the local community.

The psychological and motivational elements
(psychodynamics) of self-destructive behavior.

Legal aspects of suicide and suicidal behavior.

Characteristics of various clinical populations, such as the suicide population versus the
suicide-attempt population.

Special considerations applying to specific
age groups, such as children, adolescents and the
elderly.

Common fallacies and misconceptions about
suicide.

Characteristics of depression and the relationship of depression and other emotional disorders to the problem of suicide.

Sociological, cultural, philosophical and religious aspects of suicide.

Factors involved in the recognition, evaluation and lethality assessment of suicidal states.

The rationale of current preventive measures, intervention techniques and emergency procedures.

Referral agencies and other collaborating resources

This refers to acquaintance with the role of facilities such as the police, hospital emergency rooms, the telephone company, ambulance service, medical and social services, public health and mental health agencies, and rehabilitation resources. In other words, the worker should have knowledge of all those services which can be mobilized to help a client. Since there are frequent changes in such services (e.g. hours, fees and eligibility requirements), procedures for keeping current should also be provided all crisis workers.

Ethical considerations

This ranges from the ethics of intervention itself to the specific procedures employed to ensure confidentiality. It would include the ethics involved in such issues as limiting personal contact, tracing calls and the tape recording of calls. A number of centers now require signed statements from their workers pledging confidentiality and agreeing to each specific practice designed to assure the ethical conduct of the Center's personnel.

Record Keeping

Workers should be thoroughly instructed as to basic data they are expected to obtain, the importance of recontact information, which items of information are critical, and the purpose and value of this aspect of their work. An understanding of why workers are asked to obtain specific information will elicit greater cooperation, and this in turn will produce better data.

In summary, the worker in suicide prevention should, at the very least, be provided that factual information which will enable him to most effectively <u>recognize</u>, <u>evaluate</u> and <u>respond</u> to the person in crisis.

Specific skills and techniques to be taught include those required to achieve the following:

<u>Enable the suicide prevention worker to deal appropriately with a wide range of human problems.</u>

<u>Develop the capacity for "active listening."</u> This includes techniques for establishing rapport and trust, eliciting pertinent information, and maintaining the contact as well as the relationship.

<u>Respond effectively in emotionally charged situations.</u>

<u>Utilize suitable community resources in an efficient way.</u> That is, the techniques required to accomplish and obtain follow-up information about the referrals that are made. The more thorough the worker's knowledge of these resources, the more comfortable and sincere he can be in conveying accurate information and encouraging the client to use the recommended service. One useful means of accomplishing this is to invite representatives from referral agencies to staff meetings to discuss in detail the services they offer, and to arrange tours of psychiatric units or other facilities for the Center staff.

<u>Function within both the extent and limitations of their role as a crisis worker.</u> This includes

techniques for carrying out their responsibilities
without being "boxed in," getting involved in game-
playing, being inappropriately used, or being enticed
into such errors as personal involvement or making
unrealistic promises.

Effectively utilize consultation and backup
personnel when required during or after a call.

Implement the specific policies and practices
of the Center.

The attitudes that should be developed in a
training program include:

Acceptance of the needs of others that differ
from one's own, especially intense dependent needs.

A non-judgemental attitude toward socially
disapproved issues, such as drug abuse, unwanted
pregnancy, sexual variants, or AWOL from the military.

A realistic attitude about the role of a "helping" agent, including the extent of responsibility
and the place of guilt feelings in carrying out such
a role.

A practical yet humanistic approach to all
aspects of life, with profound respect for each
person's individuality and worthiness of esteem.

A realistic perspective regarding death, dying
and personal loss.

Since this subject matter cannot be fully developed in the course of one training period, it
is important that ongoing exposure to training activities be included in the overall program of a

Center. This is most commonly accomplished through
regularly scheduled staff meetings. Naturally the
higher the standards for the persons doing the training and for the screening and selection of workers,
the more productive the training procedures will be.

Methods Used in Training Program

The methods used in training are expected to
grow more elaborate and precise as the service gains
experience and expertise. As needs for additional
areas of training are identified, these topics --
and the methods of presenting them -- should be incorporated into the program.

This issue as far as standards are concerned
is, are appropriate methods used for each aspect of
training? Does the training program utilize effective means to convey the necessary information,
skills and attitudes essential to producing a well-
trained worker? For example, would it employ the
same style of presentation in exploring attitudes
that it would in teaching the symptoms of depression?

Training methodology lends itself to innovation
and creativity just as do other aspects of a training program. Without intending any limitation on
ways and means of achieving goals, the following
methods have been widely and effectively used, and
can provide a basis for standards in training techniques:

Written material covering all aspects of the training program.

Many centers develop a training manual which
is given to their trainees when they enter the program. Probably the best known and most widely used
is that of Farberow, Heilig and Litman (1968), at
the Los Angeles Suicide Prevention Center. This

manual has been adapted for use by a number of
centers by supplementing it with additional materials developed by the individual center.

Lecture presentations

Orientation lectures, introducing trainees to
the background, goals and purposes of a service,
are the most typical -- and efficient -- introduction to training. Lecture presentations can
also be effectively used in other parts of the
program when the instructor is called upon to share
his particular area of expertise with the trainees.

Seminars and small group presentations

Material such as individual cases illustrating
different types of problems and procedures can be
taught effectively in this way. The group should
be small enough to allow each person to express
ideas and questions freely.

Use of training aids such as tapes, films and teletrainers

While the taping of calls is still a controversial issue in many areas, the taping of calls specifically for training purposes (trainees tape
their calls, simulated or actual, for play-back
for their own review, or review with a supervisor)
is one of the most effective training aids available. Other uses of taped calls include presentation
of selected types of calls for case discussion,
tapes of repeat or problem callers, and the presentation of taped training lectures. Although most
centers can rapidly develop a supply of taped calls
which are uniquely suited to their own training
needs, some more generalized aids are available.
For example, a series of taped lectures has been
prepared by the San Francisco Suicide Prevention
Center, and is available from that center. Another

series is available from Inter/View, Inc., P.O.
Box 884, Pasadena, Ca. 91101 (Jones and Edwards),
and a third from Behavioral Sciences Tape Library,
485 Main St., Fort Lee, N.J. 07024 (Danto).

Teletrainers, special telephone training equipment that is uniquely suited to teaching telephone
techniques to suicide prevention and crisis workers,
may be obtained on loan from local telephone companies. Teletrainers are used by a number of centers and are considered to be a highly effective
training aid.

Role-playing techniques, with close supervision by
the instructor

Using this method, members of the training
staff assume the role of various types of suicidal
persons and carry on simulated crisis calls with
the trainees. The teletrainer is an excellent aid
in such role playing. This is an effective introduction to actually handling calls, and provides an
excellent opportunity to demonstrate to the trainees
the complexities involved in putting their recently
learned theories into practice.

Observation by the trainee of experienced staff
responses and dialogue with callers

The opportunity to observe senior staff workers
responding to callers and to discuss the actions
taken provide effective further training and reassurance. The trainee can observe and review each
required step, from the answering of a call to the
related paperwork and follow-up process. Trainees
should be required to observe calls until they are
thoroughly familiar with all procedures.

Handling of incoming calls independently by the
trainee, with immediate consultation available as
needed and with regular supervisory review of calls.

Ongoing training should continue indefinitely, and
readily available consultation is basic to such a
program. Another form of ongoing training and supervision would be regular review of all case reports.

In addition to the methods listed above, attention should be drawn to reading materials in
the field of suicide prevention and to the poten-
tials for continued learning through active participation in workshops, symposia and organizations
such as the American Association of Suicidology
and the International Association for Suicide Prevention.

Format of the Training Program

The specific format of a training program
will obviously vary from center to center depend-
ing on the nature of each setting. Several of the
larger centers have provided detailed reports of
each segment of their training program (Heilig,
1970; Brockopp and Yasser, 1970), which can serve
as models for new centers when designing and planning their own programs. Some pertinent questions
would be:

How long does each training class last? Established practice has somewhat arbitrarily set the
norm for duration of training. The two most common
types of scheduling are:
a) A series of all-day workshops scheduled once a
    week for from three to six weeks.
b) A series of 3-hour classes, scheduled once a
    week for six to twelve weeks.

Although there are reports of marathon training classes (one training session going on continu-
ously for two or three days), this approach is
geared more to obtaining workers in the shortest
possible time than to producing optimally trained
staff members. We still need careful studies that

compare the effectiveness of trainees who have had
widely divergent training experiences. Whatever
the pattern of scheduled training time, we consider
forty hours of instruction as a minimum total training experience before covering the phone independently.

Is the training program used as a means of
screening? Training procedures are an excellent
and necessary means of continued screening, provided this is made clear to trainees when they come
into the program. If applicants to the agency are
led to believe that admission to the training program implies acceptance into the service, then
screening out as a result of the training experience can be a devastating blow to the dismissed
trainee, as well as a source of confusion and a
detriment to the morale of those remaining. One
realistic approach to the use of training as a
means of continued screening is that used by the
Samaritans, described by Chad Varah (1967) as
follows: "The 'possibles' attend a series of
Preparation Classes (weekly for six to nine weeks)
in the form of lecture-discussions, at which un-
helpful attitudes are manifested (e.g. in the psychological problems class, those who consider the
mentally ill inferior or culpable reveal this, and
in the sexual deviations class manichaean heresies
are exposed). The 'probables' who survive the
classes are allocated to 'observation duty.' They
think this means that they observe what goes on --
as they do -- but it is so that they may be observed in action by tried and tested Samaritans who
have an uncanny knack of distinguishing the senti-
mental from the charitable, and the do-gooders from
the truly compassionate. The survivors of this are
admitted to the lowest grade, of Samaritan Helpers.
After about six months they may, if they have done
very well, be promoted to Samaritan Members."

Evaluation

The final question that must be asked is, how does a Center determine what its trainees have learned? The development of evaluating training is still in its early stages, but from a standards point of view a systematic effort to evaluate the effectiveness of training would nonetheless be considered an essential part of a well-planned training program. Because this area is least developed, there are fewer guidelines to offer.

At the least, we would look for comparisons of "before" and "after" scores on questions assessing levels of knowledge about the factual content of the training. Skills and attitudes are more difficult to measure, but even subjective evaluations by instructors, peers, supervisors and the trainees themselves give some information, as well as document the Center's efforts to develop evaluation procedures.

On a more sophisticated level, an agency could turn to the Multimedia Instructional System in Suicide Studies and Crisis Intervention, which was developed during the tenure of the Center for Studies of Suicide Prevention at the National Institute of Mental Health. This includes specialized curricula, resource materials and testing procedures, instruments and schedules. (Information is available from: Instructional System in Suicide Studies, Charles Press, 16 East 52nd Street, New York, N.Y. 10022).

Is formal instruction provided to trainees
before they are given the responsibility of responding to a caller?

How many hours are devoted overall to formal
instruction in the required training program?

Are there well worked out procedures for dropping a volunteer during the training program? For
dropping a trained volunteer who has previously
been accepted as a telephone worker?

Content -- Suicidology

Are the trainees taught:

the characteristics of depression?

how to assess lethality?

the fallacies of common misconceptions about
suicide?

theoretical approaches to life-threatening
behavior?

the sociological and cultural aspects of
life-threatening behavior?

the relationship of suicide to suicide attempts?

the legal aspects of life-threatening behavior?

the epidemiology of life-threatening behavior?

the relationship of life-threatening behavior to psychological disorders?

special considerations applicable to children, adolescents, and the elderly?

religious and philosophical concepts related to life-threatening behavior?

directions of current research in life-
threatening behavior?

crisis intervention telephone interview
techniques?

Content -- Community Resources

Are the trainees taught:

the basis for choice of available resources?

the fees, characteristics, requirements and
limitations of the principle facilities used
(especially emergency services)?

the organization of local community mental
health and public health services?

Are trainees encouraged to visit primary
resource services?

Content -- Ethical Considerations

Are the limits of responsibility of the crisis
worker clearly defined?

Are trainees fully instructed regarding procedures that insure confidentiality?

Are the limits as well as the extent of their
own relationships to callers clearly defined?

Do procedures exist in the agency regarding
deviation from prescribed practices? Any
monitoring? Disciplinary policy?

Does training deal with ethical aspects of
specific procedures such as taping, tracing
calls, or contacting police?

Content -- Record Keeping

Are trainees given specific instruction regarding the information they are to record
on each call?

Are they trained to be sufficiently familiar
with these procedures so that this task does
not interfere with the handling of the call?

Is the record-keeping aspect of their training presented in a manner that will produce
consistency and reliability in their records?

Content -- Techniques

Are trainees taught:

how to listen?

systematic techniques of intervention?

techniques of referring (elsewhere) or
transferring (to another worker) callers?

systematic techniques of assessing lethality?

techniques of securing communication with
the caller (how to reach them again)?

techniques of formulating an action plan?

systematic techniques of coping with callers'
demands for personal involvement of the
crisis worker?

techniques for systematic follow-up of
action plans, whether by contacting the
caller, referral agencies or collaterals?

Methods of Training

Is a training guide or manual provided each
trainee?

Does the guide include procedures as well as
theoretical principles?

Are trainees provided lists of referral resources?

Are pertinent pamphlets, books and reprints
made available to trainees?

Are supplementary and updated information
notices provided periodically?

What specific training methods are used, e.g.,
are films or film strips on suicide prevention
shown as part of the training?

Are tapes played to illustrate different types
of callers and differing responses? Are teletrainers and/or role-playing utilized? Are
trainees requested to tape calls for their own
playback learning experience or for review with
an instructor?

Are trainees required to observe experienced
staff members on duty before they are given
the responsibility of taking calls themselves?

Are trainees directly observed and supervised in a systematic manner when they are on duty?

Are the reports of calls <u>regularly</u> reviewed by a qualified person?

What are the procedures for discussing the quality of performance as reflected in reports, or as observed on duty by a supervisor?

Is the supervisor or professional staff available for individual discussion at the request of the trainee?

Are special educational programs provided for experienced staff members (specialists, consultants, etc.)?

Is continuing training beyond the formal program provided through such means as regular staff meetings or conferences scheduled for group discussion of callers, methods and problems?

Do staff members attend special lectures and symposia on suicide and related topics?

The subjective evaluation of responses to these questions may be used as a self-assessment check list for a given center, or may be made the basis of a "rating" by translating the responses into somewhat arbitrary values. These values can then be compared either to a predetermined absolute standard, or to the values obtained from another agency for a relative standard as compared to that agency. An example of how such a normative approach can be applied to a number of centers has been reported by Ross and Motto (1971).

BIBLIOGRAPHY

Training in suicide prevention and crisis intervention covers so broad an area that it is not feasible to provide more than a small fraction of the appropriate bibliography. For a more adequate list of resources the extensive bibliography included in the discussion by Maris, R., et al (1973), listed below, is recommended.

1. Brockopp, G., and Yasser, A.: Training the Volunteer Telephone Therapist. Crisis Intervention, 2(3):65-72,1970.

2. Farberow, N., Heilig, S., Litman, R.: Techniques in Crisis Intervention:A Training Manual. Los Angeles: Delmar Publishing Co., 1968.

3. Farberow, N.: Training in Suicide Prevention for Professional and Community Agents. Amer J Psychiatry, 125:1702-1705, 1969.

4. Heilig, S.: Training in Suicide Prevention. Bulletin of Suicidology, NIMH, No. 6, Spring, 1970, pp. 41-44.

5. Maris, R., Dorpat, T., Hathorne, B., Heilig, S., Powell, W., Stone, H., and Ward, H.: Education and Training in Suicidology for the Seventies. In: Resnik, H. and Hathorne, B. (Eds.): Suicide Prevention in the 70's. DHEW Publication No. (HSM) 72-9054, 1973.

6. Resnik, H., (Ed.): Suicidal Behavior: Diagnosis and Management. N.Y.: Little, Brown, 1968.

7. Ross, C., and Motto, J.: Implementation of Standards for Suicide Prevention Centers. Bulletin of Suicidology, NIMH, Fall, 1971, pp. 18-21.

8. Shneidman, E., Farberow, N., Litman, R.: The
    Psychology of Suicide. N.Y.: Science House,
    1970.

9. Varah, C.: The Use of Lay Volunteers in Suicide
    Prevention. Proceedings of the Fourth Inter-
    national Conference for Suicide Prevention,
    International Association for Suicide Pre-
    vention, Los Angeles, California, 1967.

10. A Social Actions Guide for Telephone Counseling.
    Department of the Air Force. Military Air-
    lift Command Pamphlet 30-7, July 3, 1973.

CHAPTER SIX

SERVICE STANDARDS

Introduction

Suicide prevention and crisis centers receive a broad spectrum of calls from individuals in every conceivable personal crisis. The expectations and needs of these callers cover a range beyond the capabilities of any single organization, and the question of what services are most needed and appropriate must be answered for each individual Center.

It is assumed that a Center's basic mode of operation includes response to crisis phone calls 24 hours a day. If clinical services are also offered, additional considerations naturally arise. Minimally the telephone service would include a) facilitating the involvement of necessary agencies when the caller has done physical harm to himself or is in danger of dying, b) referring callers to social and mental health agencies according to their specific needs, and c) providing reassurance, psychological support and an understanding listener. In the evaluation of services provided by suicide prevention centers these basic features are considered necessary, though exact criteria of excellence are difficult to establish. The process suggested here involves both direct assessment and inference from related judgments. With inherent limitations in mind, an assessment of this part of

49

a Center's service may be achieved through consideration of the following questions:

Telephone Coverage

Is the phone covered 24 hours a day? Suicide
prevention is closely tied to the concepts of
crisis intervention. It is vitally important that
immediate response be available to the individual
at moments of intense distress or when he or she
makes a spontaneous effort to reach out. The
necessity of 24-hour availability is directed to
this end. The experience of the past ten years
indicates that maximum call rates usually are
found in the late evening hours, and the frequency
of calls on weekends and holidays is disproportionately high.

Is the telephone work done in the organization's
offices? Through the use of a telephone exchange
or mechanical devices, calls may be relayed to
crisis worker's homes or other locations. This
often permits a volunteer to contribute a longer
period of time to crisis work and enables a Center
to function with a smaller staff. Some centers
have no permanent office space and all calls are
handled in this fashion. While 24-hour coverage
can be provided in this fashion, it is less effective than operating out of an established agency
office. One of the major disadvantages of in-home
crisis work is the lack of additional phones and
phone lines with which calls can be made to relatives, physicians, etc., while contact is maintained with a highly lethal caller. The crisis
worker at home also lacks the varied references,
resource lists, and referral literature which
should constitute a sizeable array of material in
a Center's offices. Also unavailable in the home
would be records of previous contacts with callers
which are highly valuable in dealing with repeat
calls, and are essential in attempting to provide

continuity of response over a period of time, by
a variety of volunteers. Those records of calls
which might be kept in the home to overcome this
disadvantage represent a potential problem as to
confidentiality of the material.

A less obvious disadvantage of home crisis
work is the environment in which the worker is taking the calls. The noise, distractions and com-
peting responsibilities of the worker's home environment (e.g., children, cooking, spouse) can make it
difficult to give complete attention to the call.
The complex and subtle nature of the psychological
interaction between caller and worker can best be
carried out in a business-like setting in which the
volunteer routinely does this work. In such a setting the volunteer is better able to monitor his
own psychological reactions, and in his relating
to the caller set aside frustrations, anger, and
concerns of everyday life. More simply stated,
away from home the volunteer can psychologically
give more of himself.

Still another advantage of taking calls in the
Center's office is the freedom from answering services or mechanical devices, which delay the re-
ception of calls and diminish the agency's control
over the all-important process of answering the
initial approach of a caller. McGee, et al (1972),
explored this issue systematically and concluded
that the level of development of an entire program
is revealed by the degree of autonomy and control
over answering the initial call. A detailed discussion of telephone equipment and its implications
for efficiency of communication with callers is
included in the survey of Fisher (1972).

Are substitutes available if a crisis worker
has a personal emergency? Procedures should be
well worked out which enable phone workers to obtain a replacement in the event they become sick

or have an emergency. It should be clearly under-
stood who has the responsibility for getting a replacement, and if the volunteer staff is large
enough a specified alternate crew may be available.
Changes in scheduling are best done by having one
person responsible for the whole task of scheduling.
This has been found to be a demanding job. In the
management of large numbers of volunteer workers
it becomes a challenge in tact and perseverance.

   Is more than one volunteer on duty at a time?
The early history of a Center will usually be typi-
fied by frantic efforts to keep the phone covered
around the clock, and the use of more than one
volunteer will be an improbable luxury. With the
passage of time a growth in staff will usually be
accompanied by an increased call rate, as the community becomes more familiar with the Center. As
the crisis staff grows, consideration should be
given to double coverage.

   The use of two telephone workers has a number
of advantages. Contact with a caller will often
generate a number of related calls. In emergencies
it is a great asset to have one worker maintain
contact with the caller while someone else summons
help, initiates a trace, contacts a neighbor, etc.
Having a fellow worker available also facilitates
making judgments about how to handle a call, through
mutual consultation.

   The use of multiple workers during periods of
high call rates enables one worker to complete supportive actions or write a report while his colleague
is taking subsequent calls. If the call rate becomes unusually high, more than one phone line
should be available. Many Centers have a business
phone number listed as well as an emergency number.
This inevitably seems to lead to the use of the
business line for crisis calls. The physical set
up of the phone equipment should be such that the

worker can readily answer calls on any phone line
to which the caller has access.

If several emergency phone lines are available,
there is an advantage in having one emergency phone
number listed and having one or more supplementary
lines linked to it. In this set up, if the primary
number is busy, the call is automatically transferred to the other line. In such an arrangement,
some provision should be made for answering the
other linked line or lines when the primary one is
busy, since the caller is not aware of the transfer
of his call and may assume that no one is there or
that the emergency number is not being answered.

The use of multiple phone lines requires phones
with push button phone line selection and typically
a hold button. In general business affairs some
people resent being placed on hold during an inter-
rupted conversation. This is an even more sensitive
issue when talking to a person in crisis and it is
advisable to have a uniform rule against putting
any caller on "hold."

It has not been systematically determined how
callers respond to an unanswered phone, but it is
not difficult to surmise, and the concepts of crisis
intervention are certainly violated by such an experience. There is an implicit element of rejection
which must be avoided. It is also not known what
reaction is elicited by a busy signal. The caller
might feel rejected in this instance also, assuming
that the agency is too busy for him. On the other
hand it might convey a positive message in that the
caller could view the busy phone line as an indication of others being in crisis and feel less set
apart from his fellow man. It appears certain that
a busy signal is preferable to an unanswered phone if
for no other reason that that the former might encourage the person to call again while the latter
would not. The number of linked crisis lines should

therefore be matched by the number of volunteers
on duty or some method of immobilizing extra lines
developed. The concern for unanswered calls is
less serious for those received on "business" phone
lines. The assumption might be that such numbers
are only active during business hours and the option
of calling the emergency number remains. Calls on
all phone lines should be taken around the clock.
The optimal coverage would be provided by at least
two volunteers scheduled 24 hours a day, with multiple crisis lines available to callers.

Referral Services

   Is information on various organizations readily
available? The training of volunteers should thoroughly familiarize them with referral procedures
and community resources, as detailed in Chapter Five.
This training should be supplemented by periodic re-
views and updating of information. The array of
possible resources is usually quite broad, and a
system for categorizing services and making this information readily retrievable by the volunteers is
important.

   Have agencies been screened and a working relationship established with frequently used resources?
Community resources should be evaluated in terms of
crisis intervention procedures and needs. The major
problem confronted here is usually accessability.
Many agencies have admission procedures and waiting
lists which make it impractical for their use on a
crisis basis. A resource should not be used solely
on the basis of the material publicized in a brochure
or general listing of services. Those agencies which
are frequently used and play a prominent role in responding to crisis should be visited by a person
designated to represent the Center, and mutual working arrangements established.

   These working arrangements may include the

designation of liaison personnel from agencies such
as hospitals, welfare programs, police, etc., to
provide personal contact and close cooperation. A
further step toward harmonious working relations
can be achieved by an interchange of in-service
training experiences between agencies. Such procedures will do much to expedite the response given
to referrals made by a suicide prevention center.

Are follow-up procedures worked out and routinely followed? The usefulness of a referral agency
is at times best determined through experience. The
practice of making follow-up contacts after a referral is very valuable both in assessing the response
of the agency and the effectiveness of the suicide
prevention center. Routine follow-up procedures
provide a check on the appropriateness of the referrals, the response biases of the callers and the
effectiveness of the volunteer in helping the caller
to utilize these agencies. Follow-up calls can be
made to either the caller or the agency to which
they were referred. Permission for such follow-up
calls should be obtained from the caller when the
initial referral is made. Experience has shown
that follow-up calls are warmly received in the vast
majority of instances and convey to the caller the
ongoing concern of the Center.

Are the private practitioners screened for
appropriateness and availability? It is quite common for callers to request or express preference
for the services of a private practitioner (physician,
psychologist, psychiatrist, social worker, minister,
school counselor). In instances where some prior
relationship has already been established, it is
generally advisable to encourage the caller to continue their use of that particular therapist. However, the challenge and responsibility presented by
the suicidal individual is not welcomed by a significant number of professionals. Even those whose
training suggests that they have particularly ap-

propriate skills in working with such problems are
not always inclined to make themselves available.
It is important to screen the private practitioners
to whom referrals are made on the basis of their
interest, as well as on their availability and
competence.

In general, of course, it is best to refer
callers to professionals who have expressed an
interest in receiving such referrals. This can
be done by sending letters of inquiry to those
professionals who meet the other criteria for referral, and enlist their cooperation. Availability
is an important factor in that some professionals
are so busy that they cannot respond with the im-
mediacy and flexibility that often is called for
in crisis situations. Determining this factor
should be accomplished in the process of establishing a referral relationship with the professionals.

The issue of competence in dealing with a suicide crisis is a sensitive one. There is a tendency
to assume competence categorically on the basis of
professional identification. While this has some
superficial logic to it, it is an unfortunate fact
that there is no guarantee of specific crisis intervention skills within any one of the many professional categories. The problem of selecting practitioners with appropriate skills may be turned over
to local professional organizations, so that the
judgment is on a peer level. Though many professional groups will be unwilling to undertake such
a selection process, it should be investigated.

Screening of professionals may also be done
by a committee within the structure of the suicide
prevention organization. It has been recommended
(Chapter Two) that centers have a Professional
Advisory Committee, and if this group is widely
representative of the various professions it would
be appropriate for it to participate in a selection
process. The results of actual experience in making

referrals should also be taken into consideration
in evaluating the usefulness of specific professionals. This may be the only procedure available,
but even if a more formal method is used in ar-
riving at a selected referral list, the experience
of the Center should be the final judgment on those
professionals used.

Effectiveness of Crisis Interveners

Are the volunteers skilled in providing psychological support? The telephone interaction can
be a very intimate and influential relationship.
The person in crisis is often quite open and vulnerable, and the impact of the crisis worker can be of
great significance. Faced with such a responsible
task the worker should know the dynamics of the
suicidal person and be able to flexibly meet a variety of stress situations. The worker should com-
municate an air of calm stability, understanding,
concern and warmth. Through training and by virtue
of his basic personality structure, the worker
should be able to exercise control in responding
to the caller's anger, depression, seductiveness
or helplessness. While the worker must retain some
objectivity and detachment, the human qualities of
concern and understanding are essential, and a Center should be more than an information booth for
emergency referrals.

The complexity of the worker's role is such
that a large amount of self-awareness is also required to properly handle calls. One of the most
frequent errors made by workers is that of letting
their own biases enter into their response to the
caller. These range from minor reactions detected
in their tone of voice to overt criticism or anger
directed to the caller. In some instances a worker
has been so pleased with some aspect of his own life
that he is unable to refrain from talking about it.
Some workers feel they are doing a noble, self-

sacrificing job and expect the callers to be ap-
preciative and respectful. The task of crisis
intervention calls upon particular strengths and
motivations, and the worker may need help in determining if he is suited for this demanding task.

The evaluation of these qualities in telephone
personnel is necessarily subjective, but can be
carried out in a systematic way. We have used four
methods:

a) Direct observation. Simply standing by
   while calls are in progress gives clues to
   the effectiveness of at least the shift
   that is working during the evaluation process.

b) Discussion of cases with volunteers. Asking about specific cases and pursuing the
   details of what was done and the underlying
   rationale permits impressions of how com-
   petent the phone workers are, without being
   restricted to calls in progress. It is
   also possible to explore in depth by posing
   hypothetical situations that demand considerable skill or intuitive sensitivity.

c) Discussion of general aspects of suicide
   prevention and crisis intervention with
   volunteers. This permits subjective impressions of warmth, responsiveness, communication skills, attitudes and motivations
   of the crisis workers. It also allows contact with a larger number of persons than
   the preceding methods.

d) Review of records. A time-honored method
   with obvious limitations, this permits an
   impression of workers who cannot be seen
   in person, by reconstructing their performance from their written reports. It also

gives information about the supervisory
process when that entails a written entry
or comments on the contact form. The need
for rapid and perceptive feedback to the
volunteer deserves emphasis in this evaluation. Precautions regarding confidentiality must be taken when written records are
made available to an outside examiner.

A fifth method, which requires a more elaborate
and time-consuming procedure but is less vulnerable
to questions of reliability and validity, is that
of formal rating scales. Still in the testing stage,
these techniques have been developed and studied by
McGee and his coworkers at the Center for Crisis
Intervention Research at the University of Florida
(McGee, R., et al, 1972). This approach focuses
on specific qualities of crisis workers, such as
technical effectiveness, clinical effectiveness,
personal characteristics and attitudes, and assessment of case outcome. Ideally, of course, these
evaluations would be used in addition to the less
refined methods now in use.

Are workers given the opportunity to discuss
their telephone experiences? A worker will experience enthusiasm, anxiety and other reactions to
phone calls which he or she will need to share.
The demands of confidentiality require that it not
be done with friends or relatives (including spouses)
and this need should be met within the agency. The
usual contacts between workers will generate some
friendships which will satisfy the need to share
these experiences, but it is also advantageous to
have formal meetings explicitly for this purpose.
The need can be partly met by setting aside time
in regular on-going training sessions for such discussions.

Are there criteria for identifying high risk
callers? Although high risk calls represent a

relatively small proportion of the total call volume, their significance gives them high priority
and the workers typically are concerned with their
ability to handle such calls. Assessing the lethality of callers is a complex and necessary skill.
There are few places in a community capable or
willing to make this judgment, and it is generally
seen as a primary function of the Suicide Prevention
and Crisis Intervention Center.

Are emergency procedures readily mobilized
by the Center? Preparation for various types of
emergencies should include a thorough knowledge of
medical facilities, availability of emergency transportation, procedures for tracing phone calls, and
special problems requiring unique resources (e.g.,
military installations, water rescue, foreign
language callers). The majority of emergencies will
be handled by a very limited number of hospital
emergency rooms. The suicide prevention center
should have direct access to these facilities, a
good understanding of their operation and a mutual-
ly agreed upon system for utilizing them. It is
often beneficial for workers to visit these facilities to learn first-hand the nature of the emergency
room setting. The caller often fears hospitaliza-
tion and it becomes part of the worker's task to
alleviate these concerns.

Additional Services

The primary mode of crisis intervention dealt
with in these discussions has been by telephone.
While this technique offers a number of advantages
and unique qualities, it is but one of several possible ways in which people in crisis can be helped.
As suicide prevention centers have developed skills
in handling crises via the telephone there has been
a movement to extend their involvement to other
forms of service. The following programs represent
a sample of these types of activities.

Outreach Program

Centers which provide an outreach activity develop a cadre of individuals who are trained and
prepared to go into the community. Such a program
greatly increases the Center's capacity to evaluate
crisis, offer support and facilitate referral. The
role of outreach personnel is more complex and requires more extensive training than the activities
of the phone worker. Some risk to personal safety
is incurred, and limits of personal involvement are
more difficult to determine and enforce.

A form of outreach activity which may be in-
creasingly used is that of follow-up of individuals
who have been discharged following a suicide attempt.
With the large number of suicide attempts coming to
the attention of emergency rooms and crisis centers,
this would represent a sizable task. There seems
little doubt, however, that the people so served
are definitely in need of care which is often not
met by their brief contact with the medical facility.
A similar outreach program might be extended to the
families of suicide victims. Here again are a significant number of individuals who may be in need
of professional care or some type of support. In
addition to the grief and burden of loss of the
loved one, they must face the misconceptions and
myths of society regarding suicide.

Psychological Autopsy

Supportive family counseling following a suicide can often be carried out in the course of conducting a psychological autopsy. This procedure
provides an excellent opportunity to a) offer direct
services to survivors and b) provide valuable data
about suicide that can increase our understanding
of self-destructive behavior in general and the
needs of the community in particular. An excellent
review of this type of service is reported by Curphey

(1967).

Community Education

Many Centers assume some responsibility for public information and professional training. In view of the pervasive lack of knowledge about suicide, these activities deserve high priority. This is often accomplished by providing speakers to schools, service clubs and interested groups. More sophisticated instruction is offered to help-giving professionals through workshops, in-service training and consultation. It has been suggested that such education and increased involvement of professionals in the social, psychological and welfare fields may have as great an impact on the prevention of suicide as any other activity.

Direct Clinical Services

A Center which has a large budget and/or a closely integrated tie with a mental health facility may offer direct clinical services. In such instances the phone worker is able to capitalize on his or her contact with a caller and involve the person with the clinical facility at hand. If trained for face-to-face counseling, the crisis worker may assume the therapist role.

Such a close knit system permits the services offered to the caller to flow with maximum continuity. The caller can utilize help offered through several modalities, and experiences less fragmentation and disruption of treatment. When affiliated clinical services are an intrinsic part of suicide prevention centers, the phone workers also have a greater sense of security and a sense of closure. It is possible for the personnel in each phase of the crisis work to offer insights and stimulation to the others, to the ultimate benefit of the client.

Special Clinical Programs

Creative approaches to supplementing the services of suicide prevention and crisis intervention centers have resulted in a wide variety of new program ideas. For example, a special telephone line for communication with elderly persons, offering of counseling to survivors of known suicides, a Youth/Drug "Hotline" service, and counseling for families of persons who are suffering from a terminal illness.

The Committee on the Delivery of Suicide and Crisis Intervention Services, of the NIMH Task Force on Suicide Prevention in the 70's, took the position that in this decade, suicide and crisis services must supplement their basic 24-hour telephone counseling and referral activity by at least a) active follow-up of every call, b) an outreach program involving direct contact with clients, and c) a variety of educational programs for the general population and for the community care-givers (McGee, et al, 1973). This presupposes a level of funding and degree of training that would be highly desirable, but is realistically a goal for optimal service rather than a minimal standard required for support of a facility. There is ample need for the basic telephone service, which in itself provides a unique resource in many communities. If the quality of its service is high, it can serve in a truly preventive role, that is, help its callers resolve conflict situations before they develop to suicidal proportions. This is a difficult function to measure but is consistent with sound public health principles and deserving of encouragement and support.

BIBLIOGRAPHY

1. Curphy, T.: The Forensic Pathologist and the Multidisciplinary Approach to Death. In: Shneidman, E. (Ed.): Essays in Self-Destruction. New York: Science House, 1967.

2. Farberow, N., Shneidman, E., Litman, R., Wold, C., Heilig, S., and Kramer, J.: Suicide Prevention Around the Clock. J Orthopsychiat 36:551-558, 1966.

3. Fisher, S.: The Voice of Hope -- To People in Crisis. Canton, Ohio: Shiela A. Fisher, 1972, pp. 47-53.

4. Fowler, D. and McGee, R.: Assessing the Performance of Telephone Crisis Workers: Development of a Technical Effectiveness Scale. NIMH Bulletin of Suicidology No.9, 1972 .

5. Haughton, A.: Suicide Prevention Programs -- The Current Scene. Amer J Psychiat 124:1692-1696, (June) 1968.

6. McGee, R., Richard, W. and Bercun, C.: A Survey of Telephone Answering Services in Suicide Prevention and Crisis Intervention Agencies. Life-Threatening Behavior 2(1):42-47 (Spring) 1972.

7. McGee, R., Knickerbocker, D., Fowler, D., Jennings, B., Ansel, E., Zelenka, M., and Marcus, S.: Evaluation of Crisis Intervention Programs and Personnel: A Summary and Critique. Life-Threatening Behavior 2(3): 168-182, (Fall) 1972.

8. McGee, R., Berg, D., Brockopp, G., Harris, J.,
   Haughton, A., Rachlis, D., Tomes, H., and
   Hoff, L.: The Delivery of Suicide and Crisis
   Intervention Services. In: Resnik, H., and
   Hathorne, B. (Eds.): Suicide Prevention in
   the 70's. DHEW Publication No. (HSM) 72-
   9054, 1973.

9. Litman, R., Farberow, N., Shneidman, E.,
   Heilig, S., and Kramer, J.: A Suicide Prevention Telephone Service. JAMA 192:21-25,
   1965.

10. A Social Actions Guide for Telephone Counseling.
    Department of the Air Force. Military Air-
    lift Command Pamphlet 30-7, July 3, 1973.

CHAPTER SEVEN

ETHICAL STANDARDS

The issue of ethics is at once the most difficult to state precisely and the most sensitive
of the areas to evaluate in a suicide prevention
and crisis intervention center. Precision is
rendered difficult by the infinite variety of situations posed to a crisis worker, and by the basi-
cally philosophical nature of the questions involved. Sensitivity is understandable in that any
criticism of ethical matters is more threatening to
a center staff than criticism of other aspects of
a center's activities. The same can be said of
the community's concerns, in that any question
about ethics would tend to overshadow the value of
whatever programs are offered. The issue is further complicated by the inflexibility that must be
exercised, since no compromise in such an area can
be comfortably tolerated.

Ethical considerations can be explored from
the standpoint of 1) operational procedures and
2) advertising, publicity and fund-raising activities. Inevitable differences of opinion will be
encountered in the interpretation of specifics,
but an evaluation can be accomplished if the basic
guidelines are clear.

Operational Procedures

A fundamental consideration is the issue of

confidentiality. Persons calling a suicide prevention center are frequently in distress about
matters of a personal nature, and it is not un-
usual for them to express concern about how the
agency handles information. Given the general
level of sensitivity and fears of callers, it is
striking to observe the amount of personal information they do divulge. This is often a tribute
to the success of the crisis workers in establishing rapport and a sense of trust with the caller.

Though one of the basic obligations of a Center is to strive to preserve human life, this must
be carried out in the context of concern for the
confidentiality, privacy and autonomy of the caller.
The freedom with which the person in crisis shares
personal information presupposes that confidentiality is respected. The caller often asks questions
regarding this issue and deserves reassurance and
genuine cooperation. This requires the thorough
training of each crisis worker in the importance
of not discussing calls outside of the agency, and
in measures to protect all personal records.

The caller's privacy includes his right to
determine the amount of information he gives, to
restrict the agency from contacting friends or relatives and to decline future contact with the agency.
In a similar vein, respect must be shown for the
individual's autonomy. By this is meant his right
to accept or reject referrals, make decisions af-
fecting his life and pursue his own life style.
When the individual, in exercising these rights,
endangers his own life, it seems only reasonable
to resolve this ethical conflict in favor of the
more basic issue of preserving life. Some practical clinical considerations in this conflict have
been discussed by Motto (1972). Much has been
written about the ethics of suicide, especially
from the point of view of the "rational" suicide
(Sprott, 1961; Choron, 1972). The important element

in this context, however, is the ethics of suicide
prevention, which requires a somewhat different
though equally controversial set of attitudes.

The crisis worker therefore must be aware of
these possible ethical conflicts and be prepared
to adapt his or her approach to the individual
circumstances. The most significant factor in
assessing the situation is the lethality of the
caller. Only the very special demands of preventing an imminent or on-going self-destructive
act should allow the worker to depart from very
strict adherence to rules of confidentiality,
privacy and autonomy.

The following questions can be used to assess
this issue:

Is the confidentiality of written records
protected? To provide a meaningful record of a
call, a report should include personal aspects of
the caller's problems as well as descriptive and
identifying data about the caller. Since a number
of crisis workers may need to refer to the report,
it is not feasible to code, abbreviate or otherwise
disguise sensitive information. This then consti-
tutes a document which could be embarrassing or
even damaging to a caller if it were seen by people
outside the agency. Caution should be taken that
call records not be left where visitors might see
them. Notes, rough drafts or other materials
which are thrown away should be screened and de-
stroyed.

Centers where calls are transferred to workers'
homes have a particularly difficult problem main-
taining the confidentiality of written records. In
many homes the phone is located for general con-
venience and probably not well suited for maintain-
ing private records. Despite the good intentions
and definite rules about how records should be

handled, the casual, informal openness of most
homes would make it difficult to keep family members away from this information.

How strict should rules of confidentiality be?
Once a person has been trained and has worked in a
suicide prevention setting for a while, he or she
develops considerable sophistication about dealing
with crisis and becomes acquainted with the complex
issues involved in considerations of life, death
and self-destruction. There is a tendency to assume that others, particularly those close to the
crisis workers, have made some sort of transition
also, and the workers are inclined to minimize the
dramatic and anxiety-producing qualities of the
calls they take. If the worker discusses a call
outside the agency because of its special interest,
the inclination to share the story may be even
stronger in the listener. The worker who gives
information to anyone, even "in confidence," is
definitely compromising the confidentiality of the
material. Crisis workers must be instructed that
they are not to discuss calls with anyone outside
of the agency, including spouses and family members.
The desire to discuss calls should be recognized,
however, and dealt with in "talk groups" or some
other informal structure within the organization.

Should calls be tape recorded? Occasionally
callers will inquire if a written record is being
made of their call but it is rare that they have
any objections to this practice when they are assured of its confidential handling. More often
the caller questions whether or not his conversation is being tape recorded and the concern about
this is more intense. It appears that a voice recording is more objectionable to the caller than
a report written by the worker. This may arise
from the fact that the written report is the prod-
uct of another person and its accuracy could be
refuted. A tape recording, on the other hand,

captures unique and personal qualities of the
caller, and its accuracy cannot be denied.

It is assumed by most suicide prevention
staffs that telling a caller that the conversation
is being recorded, or even asking permission to do
so, would lead many individuals to immediately
terminate their call. For this reason relatively
few agencies tape calls, though some Centers have
been known to record calls without prior consent
of the callers. A number of important ethical
issues are obviously raised by such a practice.
One very basic matter is that of an honest and
open relationship with the caller. The crisis
worker attempts to create an atmosphere of trust
and concern which is clearly inconsistent with
practices which deceive or mislead. It would be
necessary to establish that taping serves the
practical issue of preserving life in order to use
it in this way. Though tapes have proven to be
one of the most valuable training tools in helping
crisis workers develop self awareness, verbal skills
and sensitivity to the intervention process, it is
questionable that these benefits alone can justify
recording without the caller's knowledge. It is
not the taping but the need for consent of the
caller that raises the ethical issue.

Is taping calls legal? The decision whether
or not to tape involves legal as well as ethical
questions. Consultation with an attorney should
be used to clarify the applicable laws, which vary
in different states. If taping is done the crisis
workers should be fully informed of the issues involved and provided with the guidelines for dealing
with them.

The Committee on Taping of the American Association of Suicidology, on the basis of an extensive evaluation and nationwide survey of prac-

tices and attitudes regarding taping of client
phone calls, presented the following recommendations:

1. The practice of taping should be dis-
couraged on legal and ethical grounds as a
policy in which the potential dangers far
outweigh the potential benefits.

If despite the hazards involved a suicide prevention center intends to tape client phone calls, the following safeguards
should be scrupulously maintained:

2. The caller should be informed and informed consent should be obtained in writing.

3. If taping is done on an emergency basis,
where informed consent is not possible due
to the emotional state of the caller and the
acute life and death nature of the situation,
the tape recording should be erased as soon
as it has served its temporary emergency purpose. In no case should it be kept as a
permanent record without written consent of
the client.

4. In cases where tape recordings have been
obtained through written consent of the client for training and research purposes, all
identifying information should be erased and
the national exchange of such tape recordings
should be encouraged so as to protect privacy
and confidentiality of the clients.

5. In all cases of tape recorded conversa-
tions, whether temporary or permanent, the
strictest security measures should be employed
to protect the privacy of clients. In no
case should unauthorized persons be given access to these records.

Should calls be traced? Tracing a call from
a person who wishes to conceal his identity or
location is another practice which disregards the
preferences of the caller. The caller who is concerned with anonymity or fears that his call will
initiate some unwelcome intervention often asks
if the call is being traced. The use of sophisticated electronic devices for obtaining information,
as it is shown in the entertainment media, creates
in the general public a vague uneasiness about the
frequency with which one's privacy is invaded.
The use of tracing procedures must be considered
in the context of the caller's unwillingness or
inability to give his or her name and location.
A few instances will arise where the person has
lost consciousness or is too incapacitated to give
information, but in most cases the person will be
unwilling to do so.

The issue of ambivalence, so central to the
suicidal state in general, is clearly demonstrated
here. The person has voluntarily sought out an
agency defined as preventing suicide; he or she
is in peril but refuses to provide the information
required to complete the life-saving response. The
fundamental goal of preserving life, to which all
centers aspire, dictates that all resources be used
when a life is at stake. To not trace a call in a
life-saving situation would penalize the caller for
his or her ambivalence and disproportionately empha-
size the self-destructive aspect of the client's
dilemma. If the caller were seen as less lethal,
the importance of tracing would also be less and
the relative significance of mutual trust and the
caller's autonomy would probably negate the tracing
procedure.

What should be done with information about
illegal acts? This question invariably arises and
points to the importance of having legal consultation available to the staff. Through such consul-

tation, general guidelines should be developed for
the crisis workers and provision made for obtaining
advice on specific calls. The welfare of individuals is sometimes given greater priority than compliance with rules of confidentiality. Crimes of
violence cannot be passively recorded but any
action which is taken must consider both the legal
and mental health aspects of such actions. In no
case should the crisis worker encourage or facilitate an illegal act.

What ethical problems arise in dealing with
other agencies? Most agencies develop procedures
for meeting the ethical problems of confidentiality
and interagency communications. Those organizations
with which the suicide prevention center works most
frequently should be personally contacted and specific procedures developed for referral and exchange of information. When information is sought
from another agency, prior consent should be obtained from the caller. In general, other agencies
will respect the function of a suicide prevention
center and its need for privileged information.
The center should safeguard such information and
request it only when it is necessary to adequately
respond to the needs of the caller. In some instances an agency will have particularly stringent
requirements (e.g. a military installation), and
cooperation is usually gained through efforts to
educate and make the goals of the center relevant
to the personnel of such organizations.

Are the relationships between crisis workers
and clients strictly "professional"? In agencies
offering informal face-to-face counseling this may
sometimes be difficult to ascertain. Members of
the agency staff should not engage in primarily
social contact with callers.

Are there clear guidelines as regards the
amount, nature and handling of any fees or gifts

<u>proffered by clients</u>? The Board of Directors
should establish specific policies regulating any
type of payment. Especially sensitive are fees
charged by a paid member of the agency staff to
whom the caller has been referred.

Advertising, Publicity and Fund Raising

<u>Are the advertising, publicity and fund rais-
ing activities of the center carried out in a
manner consistent with accepted community standards,
accuracy and good taste</u>? This refers to such matters as news stories, ads, solicitation of funds,
etc. It is sometimes tempting to over dramatize
or sensationalize the life and death issues a suicide prevention and crisis intervention facility
encounters, in order to stimulate community awareness and support. Strict adherence to a matter-of-
fact approach is required to avoid any question of
making undocumented claims or unfulfillable promises.

The issue of ethics is a dynamic one which
changes with time, social development and life
circumstances. It is at once the most elusive and
yet the most sensitive ingredient in a center's
program. To establish ethical standards requires
a degree of dogmatism in an area of considerable
disagreement, especially about such areas as taping
of calls, in which distinguished voices have been
in direct opposition. Yet it is an inescapable
judgment that every crisis worker must repeatedly
make, every supervisor and consultant continually
weigh, and every agency be subjected to. If in
the final analysis suicide prevention and crisis
intervention services are found wanting, we can
take satisfaction that it will not be in this
aspect of our efforts.

BIBLIOGRAPHY

1. Choron, J.: Suicide. New York: Scribner's
      Sons, 1972, pp. 96-151.

2. Diggory, J.: Suicide and Value. In Resnik, H.:
      Suicidal Behaviors. Boston: Little Brown,
      1968, pp. 3-18.

3. Motto, J.: The Right to Suicide: A Psychiatrist's
      View. Life-Threatening Behavior 2(3):183-188,
      (Fall) 1972.

4. Sprott, S.: The English Debate on Suicide from
      Donne to Hume. LaSalle, Ill.: Open Court,
      1961.

CHAPTER EIGHT

PROGRAM EVALUATION

Not only the demand of funding agencies, but
professional pride, humanistic concern, a desire
to increase capacity and efficiency -- even a
healthy curiosity -- necessitate documentation of
an agency's effectiveness and its progress toward
specific goals. These can only be achieved by
some form of program evaluation.

Yet program evaluation continues to be a thorn
in the side of suicide prevention and crisis centers, due in large part to the number and complexity of the variables involved, uncertainty of evaluative criteria and the difficulty of interpreting
available data. The absence of a systematic plan
for evaluation of the program of a crisis center
usually reflects the extreme difficulty inherent
in both formulating and implementing such a plan.
A suggested approach to this aspect of the problem
is to be found in Appendix C.

The nature of "prevention" necessitates measuring the extent to which an event does not occur,
a difficult task at best. The vagaries of identifying and codifying suicidal deaths raise many
questions about the accuracy of measuring even those
that do occur. It is understandable, therefore,
that suicide prevention workers have generally
been inclined to either avoid the evaluative aspect
of their job or to adopt the equally questionable
expedient of simply perusing the annual suicide

76

rates published by their coroner or public health
department.

In some instances, suicide prevention workers
have been satisfied with an intuitive confidence
that what they are doing is of value, and have felt
little need to measure or even define what it is.
This may have a great deal of philosophical merit,
but will not satisfy the needs of administrative
or scientific agencies on which the suicide prevention center may depend for its continued existence.

Preliminaries to Program Evaluation

Evaluation is the process of assessing the
achievement of the stated objectives of a suicide
prevention program, and it attempts to measure the
adequacy, efficiency and acceptance of the program
by all parties concerned. Directors of suicide
prevention centers are showing an increased awareness of the need to plan and evaluate their programs in a more systematic and orderly manner than
in the past. Systematic planning of a suicide prevention program with built-in evaluation processes
offers the best hope, not only of preventing waste
but also of ensuring that the program is adhered
to and the targets reached.

An excellent discussion of this issue is provided by Roberts (1962), in which the purposes of
evaluation have been summarized thusly: "We evaluate to aid future planning and to improve programs..
to increase our understanding..to add to the body
of knowledge upon which our work is based. We
evaluate to help achieve operational efficiency
and, related to this, to obtain data that permit
interpretation of program effectiveness so as to
obtain administrative support, community support,
even financial support. We evaluate for reasons
associated with motivation -- to give staff and

volunteers satisfaction, and a sense of success.
To give priority to these purposes, I suggest that
we evaluate primarily to study the effects of practice so that we can turn our findings back into
practice and improve it and, at the same time,
strengthen the scientific basis of practice.."

If preventing self-destruction is the ultimate
goal, a sound approach dictates that we not wait
till the last straw is applied, but reach potential
suicides early in the development of a crisis situation, that is, when the lethality of the caller
is still low. There is no way of knowing how many
low lethality calls would develop into lethal situations if contact is not made early, nor how long
it would take for that transition to take place.
We can be confident, though, that low lethality
calls provide excellent opportunities for "primary"
preventive efforts, and their importance is not
diminished by the absence of immediate crisis.
Thus, measures of the readiness of the community
to utilize the suicide prevention and crisis intervention facility, as reflected by the number and
nature of calls received, can provide useful criteria for program evaluation.

Similarly, after a suicidal crisis, providing
a stabilizing influence that reduces the chances
of recurrent emergencies will likewise contribute
to the long term goal of reduced self-destruction.
A number of follow-up and outreach programs are
geared to providing such "tertiary" preventive services, and the extent of their activities can also
provide valid evaluative measures.

Of course the dramatic -- even sensational --
episodes involving police intervention or exciting
ambulance-centered events provide the most color-
ful material for evaluative data. Such literal
life-saving functions of a suicide prevention center certainly deserve recognition, but in the long

run they do not hold a more important place in the evaluative scheme than less spectacular day to day efforts.

As in other areas of risk (e.g., auto accidents), preventive programs can only reduce the overall likelihood of morbidity and mortality -- there are too many variables involved to preclude a given incident or even rate of incidents. As in the Bagley (1968) study, it is possible for an increased rate to be observed in the presence of an effective preventive influence. It only remains to be shown that in the absence of that influence the increase would have been even greater.

Sample Criteria for Program Evaluation

Based on the observations above, a set of criteria should be established that reflect both the status and progress of a given Center's program. Methods of measurement should be built into the Center's operational scheme to provide continuous monitoring of effectiveness in terms of those criteria. Periodic reassessment should be carried out as well, using criteria that are time-related, such as yearly rates of morbidity (suicide attempts) and mortality (suicides).

The following criteria are suggested as examples of program evaluation tools, which are by no means exhaustive:

Data derived from agency:

Number of calls (total calls, first party, second party, initial, repeat, return calls, elderly, adolescent, minority groups, etc.)

Number of referrals made to other agencies (number confirmed)

Crisis calls requiring police assistance

Crisis calls requiring ambulance assistance

Transportation provided

Number of referrals from community agencies, physicians, etc.

Follow-up evidence of stability -- on job, in school, functioning in home, etc.

Degree to which goal set for individual caller realized

Subjective, intuitive impressions of suicide prevention workers

Therapy program (number of clients, number of visits)

Home visit program (number, by minister, Public Health nurses, volunteers)

Data derived from population at risk:

Perceived degree of help from the suicide prevention center

Nature of help

Nature of shortcomings

Inclination to future use of suicide prevention center

Would refer someone else to suicide prevention center?

Feedback from families, e.g., where children benefited even though suicide eventually occurred

Suicide attempts after talking to suicide prevention center

How persons learned of availability of suicide prevention center

Data derived from community:

Impressions of police, social services, mental health and medical agencies

Participation of community in educational programs, symposia, volunteer activities

Participation of coroner in psychological autopsies

Suicide morbidity data from hospitals

Suicide mortality data from coroner and from Department of Public Health

Epidemiology of suicide characteristics of rates, demography, method

Standards

From the point of view of standards it is essential that a realistic program evaluation mechanism be incorporated into the overall operation of a suicide prevention and crisis center. The criteria used should be geared to the nature of the community it serves (academic, rural, industrial, urban, etc.) and provide both continuous and periodic evaluative information. This evaluative mechanism need not be an elaborate program which pretends to provide definitive proof of efficacy. Such a system has yet to be found in most areas of the behavioral sciences. Unless substantial re-

search funds and personnel are available it is not
feasible for an operating center to put the required resources into a major research effort. Examples of such studies are those of Bagley (1968),
Litman (1971) and Motto (1971).

An operating center should, however, be geared
to ongoing monitoring of all the pertinent data
that its activities generate every day, and analyzing these data with a view toward understanding
its impact on the community. It is especially
important to consider this a constantly changing
interaction, as changes in the community and development of the center's personnel and program
influence the outcome of its efforts.

Although the suicide rate is a temptingly
"objective" criterion for effectiveness (from a
strict Public Health viewpoint it is the criterion),
this measurement must not be allowed to dominate
the conceptualization of program evaluation methods.
Especially in large populations, many lives can be
saved without any appreciable effect on the apparent
suicide rate.

Some raise the issue of "efficiency," that is,
the large effort expended to save relatively few
lives. In the area of suicide, however, with the
goal of minimizing unnecessary loss of life and the
tragic impact it can have on others and on society,
we believe an old adage can be reversed, that "a
pound of prevention is worth an ounce of cure."
Indeed it appears that such a ratio is an inherent
characteristic of this work, and the untiring efforts of thousands of workers throughout the world
suggests that it is accepted as one of the realities
of suicide prevention efforts.

BIBLIOGRAPHY

1. Atkinson, M.: The Samaritans and the Elderly: Problems of Communication. Proc Fifth Internat Conf for Suic Prev, 1969, pp.159-166.

2. Bagley, C.: The Evaluation of a Suicide Prevention Scheme by an Ecological Method. Soc Sci and Med 2:1-14, 1968.

3. Bagley, C.: An Evaluation of Suicide Prevention Agencies. Life-Threat Beh 1(4):245-259, (Winter) 1971.

4. Barraclough, B., and Shea, M.: Suicide and Samaritan Clients. Lancet 2:868-870, 1970.

5. Breed, W. (Workshop Leader): Program Evaluation for Suicide Prevention Centers. In Proceedings, Suicide Prevention - Advanced Workshop, Univ of California (S.F.) Medical Center, March, 1970. (Suicide Prevention Center of San Mateo County, California, Charlotte Ross, Exec. Dir.).

6. Diekstra, R., and van de Loo, K., (Eds.): The Cost of Crisis. Assen (The Netherlands): van Gorcum, 1973.

7. Diggory, J.: Calculation of Some Costs of Suicide Prevention Using Certain Predictors of Suicidal Behavior. Psychol Bull 71(5): 373-386, 1969.

8. Green, S., and Bagley, C.: Effect of Psychiatric Intervention in Attempted Suicide. Brit Med J 1:310-312, Feb 6, 1971.

9. Litman, R.: Suicide Prevention Center Patients: A Followup Study. NIMH Bull of Suicidology, (Spring) 1970, pp. 12-17.

10. Litman, R.: Suicide Prevention: Evaluating Effectiveness. Life-Threat Beh 1(3):155-162, (Fall) 1971.

11. Litman, R., and Farberow, N.: Evaluating the Effectiveness of Suicide Prevention. Proc 5th Internat Conf for Suicide Prevention, London, 1969, pp. 246-250.

12. McGee, R., et al: Evaluation of Crisis Intervention Programs and Personnel: Summary and Critique. Life-Threat Beh 2(3):168-182, (Fall) 1972.

13. Motto, J.: Evaluation of a Suicide Prevention Center by Sampling the Population at Risk. Life-Threat Beh 1(1):18-22, (Spring) 1971.

14. Roberts, B.: Concepts and Methods of Evaluation in Health Education. Internat J Health Educ 5(2):52-62, 1962.

15. Sawyer, J., Sudak, H., and Hall, S.: A Followup Study of 53 Suicides Known to a Suicide Prevention Center. Life-Threat Beh 2(4):227-238, (Winter) 1972.

16. Schulman, R.: Suicide and Suicide Prevention: A Legal Analysis. Amer Bar Assoc J 54:855-862, 1968.

17. Suchman, E.: Evaluative Research. Baltimore, Penguin Books, 1964.

18. Walk, B.: Suicide and Community Care. Brit J Psychiat 113:1381-1391, 1967.

19. Weiner, I.: The Effectiveness of a Suicide
    Prevention Program. Mental Hygiene
    53(3):357-363, July, 1969.

20. Zusman, J., and Ross, E.: Evaluation of the
    Quality of Mental Health Services. Arch
    Gen Psychiat 20:352-257, 1969.

APPENDIX

CHECK LIST
OF
MANAGEMENT PRACTICES AND PROGRAM

I. <u>Objectives of Agency</u>   <u>Yes</u>   <u>No</u>

The agency incorporation papers or
other formal documents delineate the
following:

1. Purpose, aims and goals of the
   agency .... ____ ____
2. A statement of the charitable
   nature of the agency........... ____ ____
3. The type of clientele the agency
   is to serve.................... ____ ____
4. The quality of professional ser-
   vices to be rendered........... ____ ____
5. The intended goals of service
   provided....................... ____ ____
6. The following programs require
   license to operate -- Specify:
   Program_____Authority_____
   Valid License_____
7. The Agency is classified as <u>not</u>
   a private foundation as defined
   in Section 509 (a) of the Internal
   Revenue Code................... ____ ___
8. If Agency is receiving federal
   grants for program, does it file
   Employee Information Report EEO-1,
   (Equal Employment Opportunity
   Commission).................... ____ ___

II. Governing Authority   Yes   No

9. There is a designated authority
   to govern the agency........... ____ ____
10. Organization of this authority
    is set forth in writing........ ____ ____
11. By-Laws have been adopted...... ____ ____
    If Yes, they include:
    a. Requirements for membership. ____ ____
    b. Method for election/ap-
       pointment of members........ ____ ____
    c. Method for election/ap-
       pointment of officers....... ____ ____
    d. Provision for rotation of
       members on Board of
       Directors................... ____ ____
    e. Provision for compensation
       to Board members............ ____ ____
    f. Provision for standing com-
       mittees..................... ____ ____
       If Yes, they include:
       1. Finance................... ____ ____
       2. Personnel................. ____ ____
       3. Program.................. ____ ____
       4. Other (list)_____

Accountability of Manangment

12. The governing authority has for-
    mally established the authority
    delegated to the executive
    director...................... ____ ____
13. An independent audit of finan-
    cial operations is made annual-
    ly............................ ____ ____
14. The governing authority formally
    selects the independent auditor ____ ____
15. The financial audit is transmit-
    ted directly to the governing
    authority prior to submission
    to the funding agency.......... ____ ____

	Yes	No

16. The Executive Director or his
designated representative
routinely attends:
a. Meetings of the governing
authority.................. ____ ____
b. Meetings of committees of
the governing authority.... ____ ____
c. Appropriate meetings of
other welfare service agencies and public bodies concerned with the agency's
field of service........... ____ ____
17. The management of the agency is
based on a written plan of
operation..................... ____ ____
18. There are statements of functions and assigned responsibilities...................... ____ ____
19. Accountability of auxiliary or
fund raising groups is de-
fined......................... ____ ____

III. Fiscal Operations

20. Agency operates from a written
budget approved by the Board
of Directors.................. ____ ____
21. Executive Director on a regular periodic basis analyzes
and records variances in the
agency's budget............... ____ ____
22. A monthly financial statement
related to the approved budget is presented to the Board
of Directors at its regular
meetings...................... ____ ____
23. There is an annual inventory
of agency property............ ____ ____

24. There is a regular program for
    maintenance of buildings and
    equipment...................... _____ ____
    Buildings are owned_____, or
    leased_____.
25. There are regular policies on
    the use of reserve funds...... _____ ____

IV. Planning Activities

26. There is a written long-range
    plan for agency development... _____ ____
27. There is a written short-range
    plan for agency development... _____ ____
    Written plans include:
28. Priority of objectives........ _____ ____
29. Time period for achievement... _____ ____
30. Character of area such as the
    following:
    a. Socio-economic character-
       istics..................... _____ ____
    b. Demographic trends......... _____ ____
    c. Condition of housing struc-
       ture....................... _____ ____
    d. Alternate sources of ser-
       vice....................... _____ ____
       Such as:
31. Agency prepares and disseminates
    an annual report.............. _____ ____
    If Yes, it includes:
    a. Agency organization........ _____ ____
    b. Description of service pro-
       grams...................... _____ ____
    c. Financial summary of oper-
       ations in accordance with
       national standards......... _____ ____

V. Service Effectiveness   Yes   No

32. There is a written statement
approved by the Board of
Directors regarding procedures
for measuring service effective-
ness...................................____ ____
If Yes, evaluation method is:
a. Informal -
   1) Staff evaluation of pro-
      gram accomplishments.....____ ____
   2) Informal client
      (constituent feedback)...____ ____
b. Intermediate -
   1) Periodic evaluation by a
      national standard setting
      organization.............____ ____
c. Formal evaluative research
   study by outside consultants____ ____
33. Board of Directors receives reports regarding impact of services in realizing agency objectives......................____ ____

VI. Personnel Administration

34. There is a written document
proved by the Board of Directors setting forth personnel
policies......................____ ____
If Yes, it includes the policy
for:
a. Hours of work..............____ ____
b. Promotions.................____ ____
c. Employee health services...____ ____
d. Sick leave.................____ ____
e. Vacations..................____ ____
f. Termination of employment..____ ____
g. Employee grievances........____ ____
35. Each employee is issued a copy
of the personnel policies.....____ ____

Yes No

36. Personnel policies and practices are reviewed with each
new employee................ ____ ____
37. There are written job descriptions covering all
positions.................... ____ ____
38. There is a written position
evaluation process.......... ____ ____
39. There are operational or pro-
cedural manuals of agency
functions made available to
personnel.................... ____ ____

VII. Purchasing and Inventory Management

40. Written purchasing policies
are in use.................. ____ ____
They include:
a) An approval system for pro-
curement of capital items ____ ____
b) An approval system for all
purchases................ ____ ____
c) A statement of the persons
authorized to contract for
the agency............... ____ ____
41. The purchasing system and
records include:
a) A written purchase re-
quest..................... ____ ____
b) Price quotes/bids from two
or more sources.......... ____ ____
c) A written purchase order. ____ ____
d) A reviewing report veri-
fying quantity and quality
of receipts.............. ____ ____
e) Separation of ordering/re-
ceiving functions........ ____ ____

VIII. Insurance Protection

   42. The agency has protected it-
      self with insurance.........____ ____
      It includes:
      a) Fire with extended cover-
         age......................____ ____
      b) Fire only...............____ ____
      c) Water damage............____ ____
      d) Smoke damage............____ ____
      e) Liability damage........____ ____
      f) Comprehensive coverage...____ ____
      g) Owners, landlord and
         tenants liability........____ ____
      h) Professional acts of the
         staff....................____ ____

AGENCY NAME:_____

PREPARED BY:_____TITLE:_____

DATE:_____

APPENDIX B

DESIRABLE TRAITS IN VOLUNTEERS

1. A real desire to be of help to another individual...(persons who have fantasies of being a god or a hero are disenchanted quickly).
2. Ability to read others feelings.
3. Compassion.
4. Non-judgemental attitude. A sincere liking
   of other people and willingness to try to
   understand them without judging, and can hope-
   fully project this warmth and feeling over
   the telephone to callers. This helps with
   fellow workers too.
5. Punctuality.
6. Dependability (factors such as having many
   young children who frequently make unexpected
   demands, having a spouse who objects to membership in S.P.C., ill health, etc., may interfere
   with dependability).
7. At least average I.Q. (there doesn't seem to
   be any particular advantage to the volunteer's
   having superior intelligence unless he is willing to use it).
8. Good physical health.
9. Emotional stability.
10. Emotional maturity. Patience -- an ability to
    take many long hours of boredom. This is
    needed for those shifts which have very few
    calls from suicidal people, or, in fact, calls
    of any kind. All shifts are like this at times.
11. Endurance, an ability to tolerate pressure --
    especially emotional pressure.

12. Low anxiety -- plus ability to remain "cool" in emotionally laden situations.
13. Cheerfulness and good sense of humor.
14. A liking for order (we need good orderly records -- sometimes which involve detail. Volunteers who refuse to cooperate in this way invariably cause hardships for someone else).
15. Willingness to cooperate within the framework of established procedures; the supervisory system.
16. Willingness to learn (this would include good attendance at training meetings and seminars as well as willingness to keep up with new instructive materials).
17. Willingness to do more than serve a 4-hour shift. Sincere desire to work with S.P.C.
18. Respect for others (this would include respect for the privacy of our callers and our volunteers as well as respect for the S.P.C. organization as a whole).
19. Willingness and cooperativeness in undergoing screening.
20. A healthy dab of optimism.
21. A tolerance for frustration (the frustration of calls which end in the middle, of calls which never come, of referrals which are accepted but never acted on and the frustration of never knowing what happens to some calls or learning that the agency involved was not able to cope).
22. An ability to recognize their own limitations to help persons.
23. An ability or freedom to talk about death without having to moralize.
24. Some insight into one's own personality and problems, and a willingness to look at one's faults, accept same, and changing if and when possible.

UNDESIRABLE TRAITS IN VOLUNTEERS

1. Having the idea that S.P.C. work involves dramatic, suspenseful rescues by hero-like volunteers.
2. Having the idea that there are certain cases which only they can handle or understand.
3. Lack of insight into their own and others feelings and motives.
4. Judgmental attitudes, extreme moralism or religiosity.
5. Tardiness -- they do not report for shifts on time.
6. Undependability (failing to appear for duty without notifying anyone; failing to perform assigned tasks; failing to do what they promise that they will do).
7. Less than average intelligence.
8. Physical illness.
9. Alcoholism or being an addictive personality.
10. Having insatiable needs for attention and recognition.
11. Depression -- some moderately depressed volunteers want to work through their depression by overworking on the phone.
12. High anxiety and low tolerance for stress (low endurance).
13. Immaturity.
14. Dislike for order in record keeping and information gathering.
15. Unwillingness to cooperate with other volunteers and supervisors; unwillingness to follow procedures or to check with supervisors whenever they feel procedures should be forgotten.
16. Inability to take criticism -- reacts to all criticism as if it were negative criticism.
17. Inability to discuss certain topics such as homosexuality or obscene callers.

18. Senility.
19. Lack of self control of sexual urges; sexual acting out with other volunteers or people calling S.P.C.
20. Psychosis or sociopathic behavior.
21. Destructiveness...(this refers to persons who are jealous and critical to the point that morale begins to be affected -- their aim seems to be to destroy, for they show no willingness to think of workable solutions to the problems they unearth).
22. Failure to appear at testing sessions or scheduled meetings.

APPENDIX C

PROGRAM EVALUATION -- FROM CONCEPT TO ACTION

I. What is program evaluation? It is that part
of program management having to do with measuring and valuing programs. It includes:

    A. The association of accomplishments with
stated goals in order to arrive at sound
program decisions.

    B. The determination of whether available
resources are allocated in the best way to
optimize results in achieving recognized
objectives.

    C. The asking of basic -- and sometimes un-
pleasant -- questions about programs, to
make certain they _will_ or _do_ meet public
needs.

    D. The possible application of research tools,
such as experimental and control groups, to
help in analyzing program accomplishment.

II. Why do we need program evaluation? In short,
to help make decisions -- decisions to modify,
to expand, to curtail, to continue, or to terminate programs.

    A. Service agencies have a responsibility to
society to see that the most and best service possible is being rendered, and that
programs meet genuine social needs.

    B. The need for a given program may change with
the passage of time. Consequently, there

should be a continuing analysis of each program from the standpoint of need, objective,
and alternate ways of accomplishing its objectives.
C. Occasional programs are launched which are
not really needed, and there is a strong
tendency for programs, once started, to be
carried along without being seriously ques-
tioned.
D. Without program evaluation there is no way
of knowing or documenting that public activities are in fact achieving program objectives.
E. Evaluation assists the program administrator
to demonstrate to all concerned that the
program is achieving its objectives.

III. What is the relationship between program evaluation and performance standards?

A. Standards often reflect activity rather than
accomplishment.
B. Too often performance standards are adopted
before the agency has clarified its objectives, so that the standards have little
meaning.
C. Performance standards that are drawn carefully and related to objectives can be useful in appraising program accomplishment.

IV. What are some of the factors that inhibit program evaluation?

A. In many cases, programs are not identified
clearly and objectives are not well defined.
B. Some programs, by their very nature, are
difficult to evaluate (e.g., research, creative, or analytical jobs).
C. Evaluation often leads to change. Many
people feel threatened by change and are
concerned about how it will affect their

jobs, status, or reputation.
D. There is little real reward for program
   evaluation. If you don't "rock the boat,"
   nothing will happen; if you do, you will
   probably get nothing out of it but lumps.
   Your staff will feel that you have deserted
   them; pressure groups will descend on you,
   and your board will be unhappy because you
   caused all this trouble.
E. Evaluation requires time, energy, and understanding. These "cut into" operations.
F. Management inadequacy or poor supervision
   can seldom bring about program evaluation.

V. Who is responsible for program evaluation?

A. Evaluating a program goes on constantly by
   a whole host of viewers, all the way from
   the workers on the firing line up through
   various levels of jurisdiction; by the client, and ultimately by the sponsoring agency.
   Measuring is most usually done by the program unit.
B. Overall responsibility rests with those
   charged with administration of the unit.
C. Actual and direct responsibility rests with
   persons at each level to carry out evaluation of programs for which they have responsibility.

VI. How simple or how complex should program evalu-
    ation be?

A. Program evaluation of an informal, impression-
   istic nature goes on all the time -- largely
   undocumented.
B. The nature of the program often determines
   how complex a formal evaluation can be.
C. The program director should aim at presenting
   evidence of a kind from which a reasonable
   man can draw conclusions; evidence to convince

an average person.
D. The formal evaluation process need not cover
the entire range of program accomplishments,
but the evaluation sample ought to be carefully selected to reflect the most meaningful, the more pertinent aspects and activities.
E. The accomplishment or non-accomplishment of
short-term objectives can often indicate
the probability of success in achieving long-
term goals.

VII. What are the steps in program evaluation? Evaluation always takes place, oftentimes unbeknown
to the people who really ought to be informed.
If it is to serve a constructive purpose, program evaluation MUST BE BUILT IN! The program
director is the central point for this "build-
ing in" process.

The following are suggested steps for formulating an evaluation plan:

A. Evaluation does not take place in a vacuum --
   1. Develop a clear statement of the need the
      program is designed to meet or the problem
      it is intended to solve (goals).
   2. Determine what you want to accomplish in
      order to bring this about (objectives).
   3. Restate your goals and objectives, in
      writing, in measurable terms, whenever
      possible.
B. Don't expect it to be easy -- many barriers
   exist --
   4. Specify Evaluation as one of your program
      objectives.
   5. Describe the activities which must occur
      to achieve the objectives, including the
      activity of evaluation; include target
      dates.

6. Estimate and show the resources required to carry out activities.

C. Evaluation "threatens" individuals --
7. Involve all staff members in the evaluation process.
8. Keep your staff informed of progress and results.

D. Consider your audience and your critics --
9. Inventory those with a significant role in evaluation.
10. Anticipate nature of evidence needed.

E. Informed judgments require data --
11. Decide on evidence you are willing to be judged on or by.
12. "Build in" methods for recording and reporting essential data.
13. Maintain surveillance and control.

F. Remember a picture is worth many words --
14. Prepare and present evidence in the most understandable form and format.

G. The ultimate purpose of evaluation is to help decision makers to decide on modification, elimination or continuation of a program.
15. Prepare recommendations and proposals.
16. Associate proposals with evaluation analysis; show modifications and desired changes.

VIII. What steps might be taken to stimulate program evaluation?

A. The sponsoring organization should make clear to the board of directors and the executive director that they are expected to carry on program evaluation efforts.

B. Give special recognition to those who show evidence of having accomplished some real program evaluation.

C. Recast the budget document in program terms, since one of the first essentials in con-

ducting program evaluation is program
identification.
D. Consider instituting an annual reporting
system on program changes.
E. Carry on training activities to develop
understanding and increase interest in
program management.

INDEX

NAME INDEX

Ansel, E., 64
Atkinson, M., 83

Bagley, C., 79, 82, 83
Barraclough, B., 83
Bercun, C., 64
Berg, D., 8
Breed, W., 83
Brockopp, G., 8, 9, 47

Choron, J., 67, 75
Curphey, T., 61, 64

Davidson, D., 9
Diekstra, R., 83
Diggory, J., 75, 83
Dorpat, T., 47

Farberow, N., 30, 36, 47,
   48, 64, 84
Fisher, S., 17, 18, 64
Fowler, D., 64

Green, S., 83

Hall, S., 84
Harris, J., 8
Harvey, G.,
Hathorne, B., 8, 47
Haughton, A.,   , 8, 64
Heilig, S., 29, 30, 36,
   47, 64
Herring, J., 14, 18
Hoff, L., 8

Jennings, B., 64

Knickerbocker, D., 64
Kramer, J., 64

Litman, R., 30, 36, 47,
   48, 64, 82, 84
Loeb, A.,x

Marcus, S., 64
Maris, R., 47
McGee, R., 8, 29, 30, 59,
   63, 64, 84
Motto, J., 46, 47, 67,
   75, 82, 84

Powell, W., 47
Pretzel, P., 30

Rachlis, D., 8
Randell, J., 30
Resnik, H., 8, 47, 75
Richard, W., 64
Roberts, B., 77, 84
Ross, C., 46, 47
Ross, E., 85

Sawyer, J., 84
Schulman, R., 84
Shea, M., 83
Shneidman, E., 30, 48, 64
Sprott, S., 67, 75
Steinberg, J.,x
Stone, H., 47
Suchman, E., 84
Sudak, H., 84

Tomes, H., 8

Van de Loo, K., 83
Varah, C., 29, 30, 40, 48

Walk, B., 84
Ward, H., 47

109

SUBJECT INDEX